BestMasters

Mit „**BestMasters**" zeichnet Springer die besten Masterarbeiten aus, die an renommierten Hochschulen in Deutschland, Österreich und der Schweiz entstanden sind. Die mit Höchstnote ausgezeichneten Arbeiten wurden durch Gutachter zur Veröffentlichung empfohlen und behandeln aktuelle Themen aus unterschiedlichen Fachgebieten der Naturwissenschaften, Psychologie, Sozialwissenschaften, Technik und Wirtschaftswissenschaften. Die Reihe wendet sich an Praktiker und Wissenschaftler gleichermaßen und soll insbesondere auch Nachwuchswissenschaftlern Orientierung geben.

Springer awards **"BestMasters"** to the best master's theses which have been completed at renowned Universities in Germany, Austria, and Switzerland. The studies received highest marks and were recommended for publication by supervisors. They address current issues from various fields of research in natural sciences, psychology, social sciences, technology, and economics. The series addresses practitioners as well as scientists and, in particular, offers guidance for early stage researchers.

Caroline Dominik

Embedding Sequential Circuits for their Polynomial Formal Verification

Springer Vieweg

Caroline Dominik
University of Bremen
Bremen, Germany

ISSN 2625-3577   ISSN 2625-3615   (electronic)
BestMasters
ISBN 978-3-658-50154-9   ISBN 978-3-658-50155-6   (eBook)
https://doi.org/10.1007/978-3-658-50155-6

This Springer Vieweg imprint is published by the registered company Springer Fachmedien Wiesbaden GmbH, part of Springer Nature.
The registered company address is: Abraham-Lincoln-Str. 46, 65189 Wiesbaden, Germany

If disposing of this product, please recycle the paper.

Preamble

Over the past several decades, the scale and intricacy of modern circuits have expanded at an astonishing pace. Early processors from the 1970s contained only a few thousand components, whereas today's cutting-edge devices integrate over 100 billion elements. Beyond this raw complexity, the design of *Cyber-Physical Systems* (CPS) adds another dimension, requiring close consideration of how systems interact with their physical environments.

The past 30 years have seen remarkable progress in design methodologies, culminating in the highly automated design flows now standard in the *Electronic Design Automation* (EDA) industry. Initially, the primary goal of EDA was straightforward: to realize a given specification using as few components as possible—optimizing for minimal area and high performance through shallow circuit depth.

However, design objectives have since broadened significantly. As electronic systems are increasingly deployed in safety-critical domains—such as automotive or aerospace applications—the long-term reliability and correctness of circuits have taken center stage. This shift calls for advanced verification strategies capable of ensuring functional correctness not just at the moment of production, but across the entire operational lifespan of a device.

Traditional simulation and emulation techniques, while effective in simpler scenarios, fall short in the face of modern system complexity. To address this, formal verification methods have gained prominence, as they enable rigorous mathematical proofs of correctness. Nonetheless, the inherent exponential complexity in both runtime and memory usage poses serious scalability challenges for formal verification when applied to large designs.

To bridge this gap, *Polynomial Formal Verification* (PFV) has emerged as a promising new paradigm. PFV techniques offer provable upper bounds on verification complexity, thereby making it feasible to verify complete systems efficiently and effectively.

This book represents a meaningful contribution to this evolving field. It is based on the master's thesis of Caroline Dominik, developed during her time with the *Group of Computer Architecture* (AGRA) at the University of Bremen, Germany.

While PFV was successfully applied to combinational circuits, like ad-ders and multipliers before, in her thesis she showed for the first time that this con-cept can also be extended to sequential circuits, i.e., circuits containing memory elements. Her studies show the surprising result that also circuits that have an exponential sequential depth, like counters, can be fully checked for correctness using formal proof techniques within polynomial bounds.

The quality of her findings is also confirmed by a publication at an inter-national conference in the field, that resulted from the thesis: Polynomial Formal Verification of Sequential Circuits. *Design, Automation & Test in Europe Conference & Exhibition (DATE 2024)*, Valencia, Spain, 2024.

I hope you will enjoy reading this book.

Bremen   Prof. Dr. Rolf Drechsler
June 2025   drechsler@uni-bremen.de

Contents

List of Acronyms

AGRA	Group of Computer Architecture
ALU	Arithmetic Logic Unit
ASP	Answer Set Programming
BDD	Binary Decision Diagram
BMC	Bounded Model Checking
*BMD	Multiplicative Binary Moment Diagram
CEC	Combinational Equivalence Checking
EDA	Electronic Design Automation
FSM	Finite State Machine
LSB	Least Significant Bit
MSB	Most Significant Bit
PFV	Polynomial Formal Verification
RDMC	Restricted Domain Model Checking
SAT	Boolean Satisfiability Problem
SCA	Symbolic Computer Algebra
SEC	Sequential Equivalence Checking
SMC	Symbolic Model Checking
SRA	Symbolic Reachability Analysis

List of Figures

List of Tables

Introduction

It is a common practice to utilize well established concepts in a different context. For instance, one can think of many examples, where something made by humans imitates nature:

- Over millions of years of evolution the shape of birds has adapted itself to flying, hence it is imitated when building an airplane.
- Honeycomb structures, which are built by bees, are often used when lightweight and stable structures are needed, e.g. in the automotive industry or as packaging material.
- A popular example in the area of computer science are of course neural networks, which imitate the neurons in a brain.

Such adaptations can be encountered in the hardware domain as well. A method used for combinational circuits, which compute a function that only depends on the inputs to the circuits, is often adapted to be applied to sequential circuits, which further depend on the state of internal memory elements. The verification of a hardware design aims to check if the design fulfills its specification. A common approach is to compare two circuits, e.g. a well established design and an optimized version of it. This is called *Combinational Equivalence Checking* (CEC) and is often done with a miter circuit [1], which compares the outputs of both circuits for several input patterns. This **well-known method has been adapted**, to be applied to the sequential version of the problem. For *Sequential Equivalence Checking* (SEC), sequences of input patterns are applied to the miter circuit. Such an adaption of an established method is proposed in this thesis as well.

The already mentioned simulation of a circuit design only achieves complete verification, if every possible input pattern or sequence of input patterns is tried. It is well known that the state space of modern systems renders this advance unimagin-

C. Dominik, *Embedding Sequential Circuits for their Polynomial Formal Verification*, BestMasters, https://doi.org/10.1007/978-3-658-50155-6_1

able. Instead, **formal methods are needed to mathematically prove the complete correctness** of safety-critical systems. Formal verification has gained significance in the industrial design flow of hardware [2], but central challenges still have to be overcome for a broad application. An essential aspect is the unpredictability of resource demands occurring during the verification. Most manufacturers cannot afford a blow-up in the required memory or time. But the computational complexity of the underlying problems shows that such an explosion in resources is possible:

- It is well known that the *Boolean Satisfiability Problem* (SAT), which determines if a formula is a tautology, is NP-complete [3]. Since CEC can be reduced to checking a miter circuit for SAT, it is coNP-complete.
- Boolean *Symbolic Reachability Analysis* (SRA) verifies a sequential circuit based on a model abstracting when the circuit passes from one state to another. This model is used, to determine which states the circuits can acquire. It is computationally even harder with PSPACE-complete (see Chap. 4 of [4]).

This challenge is addressed by *Polynomial Formal Verification* (PFV). Different verification methods and classes of circuits are analyzed in detail, to proof polynomial upper bounds for the time and space resources needed throughout the entire verification process of selected use cases. That way, **PFV ensures an efficient verification** for the chosen type of circuit. This concept has already been successfully applied to several combinational circuits [5][6][7][8][9]. But **PFV of sequential circuits has barely been considered so far**. In [10] it was only proven for a very limited sequential depth, meaning only a short sequence of inputs was relevant for the considered circuit. But in [11] PFV could be proven for n-bit full counter circuits counting up to $2^n - 1$. With that, **verification within polynomial resource restrictions was proven for an exponential sequential depth for the very first time**. But while full counter circuits were completely covered by this proof, it only included some modulo counters, which are counters that count up to any value between 1 and $2^n - 1$. The proposed method was mainly suited to verify bijective functions, which does not apply for modulo counters. This limitation is eliminated within this thesis, by adapting an established method of a different domain for the use case of PFV.

   The borrowed method has its origin in the domain of reversible computation [12]. This includes all functions, for which the corresponding input pattern can always be derived based on any output pattern. One of the main use cases of this development is low power design. This is based on the observation that any loss of information during a computation always results in energy dissipation [13]. Therefore, the functions have to be bijective, if their energy loss is supposed to be reduced [14]. This circumstance could give direction to the development of improved chips, because increasing the number of transistors in a circuit while maintaining its size is limited by the heat dissipation a circuit can withstand. Reversible computation is used for quantum computing as well, because the computations of a quantum circuit are always reversible. Other applications are e.g. optical computing or nanotechnologies. But most functions are not reversible ones. Hence, the concept of embedding is central within the aforementioned application domains. **Embedding an irreversible function aims to turn it into a reversible one**, which makes it usable e.g. for using it in a low power design.

Within this book, the embedding method is utilized for the efficient formal verification of modulo counters. As mentioned, the verification method proposed in [11] is suited for bijective functions and modulo counters are not bijective—embedding can bridge this gap. Therefore, the method of [11] is extended in this thesis by adapting the embedding concept of reversible computation. The process of formally verifying full counters and modulo counters is analyzed based on this extended method. Polynomial upper bounds for the resource requirements are calculated, so that PFV can be proven for both types of circuits. Further, the verification process is implemented, so that these theoretical bounds can be confirmed by experimental results. With this, the book aims to **provide a first, complete approach to the efficient formal verification of sequential circuits with an exponential sequential depth**.

The structure of the thesis is explained in the following. As a foundation for all following reasoning, a more thorough explanation of PFV is given in Chap. 2 and the necessary concepts are defined in Chap. 3. The PFV of full counter circuits is explained in Chap. 4 and extended by the concept of embedding to proof PFV of modulo counter circuits in Chap. 5. The results are underlined by experiments in Chap. 6. Finally, the thesis is concluded in Chap. 7.

Polynomial Formal Verification

2

This section aims to give a more detailed insight into the idea of PFV and the achievements, that have been accomplished in that area so far. This is done by first motivating the approach and giving options on how to address a proof for PFV. Then some examples for PFV of combinational and sequential circuits are given.

2.1 Motivating the Concept

To maximize the quality of a system, an important step of the development process is to verify the hardware design. But considering the enormous size of modern designs, explicitly applying every possible input pattern to verify the result is far from feasible. Hence, formal methods are necessary if the correctness of a circuit design is supposed to be proven for its entire functionality.

To implicitly argue about all possible input patterns of a system, **symbolic simulation** [15] can be used. Instead of explicit values, variables are applied to the inputs and propagated throughout the circuit in the same manner. Based on these symbolic values the simulation acquires the function computed by the circuit instead of one specific output pattern.

The efficiency of this process can depend on how this function is represented. Storing it as a *Binary Decision Diagram* (BDD) can greatly accelerate the computation. Already in 1986 in [16] instances of an *Arithmetic Logic Unit* (ALU) with up to 64 bits were verified based on BDDs. Then this would not have been feasible for more than 8 bits if based on truth tables, with advancements in technology the statement would probably hold for 16 bits today. On the other side, the size of a BDD representing an integer multiplier has been shown in [16] to always be exponential with respect to the size of the inputs. But the requirements for PFV go even further than that. Even if the final result of a considered circuit can be represented

© The Author(s), under exclusive license to Springer Fachmedien Wiesbaden GmbH, part of Springer Nature 2026
C. Dominik, *Embedding Sequential Circuits for their Polynomial Formal Verification*, BestMasters, https://doi.org/10.1007/978-3-658-50155-6_2

within polynomial bounds, that alone would not be sufficient. The **entire verification process** has to be considered to prove that a design can be verified efficiently. Otherwise intermediate blow-ups in the resource demands can occur.

Example 2.1 *Consider a miter circuit [1] as depicted in Fig. 2.1. It compares two circuits A and B for CEC. The same n inputs are applied to both circuits and each output of A is passed on to an XOR-gate together with its counterpart of B. All results are combined by an OR-gate. If the output of this final gate is equal to "0" for all input patterns, both circuits A and B compute the same function. This can be checked by the symbolic simulation of the miter circuit. If the comparison succeeds, the BDD for the final result is the constant "0". But it is easy to see that the intermediate BDDs, describing the outputs of gates in either of the circuits or of the XOR-gates, must be bigger than that. Hence, simply analyzing the size of the final result is not a sufficient basis to prove PFV.*

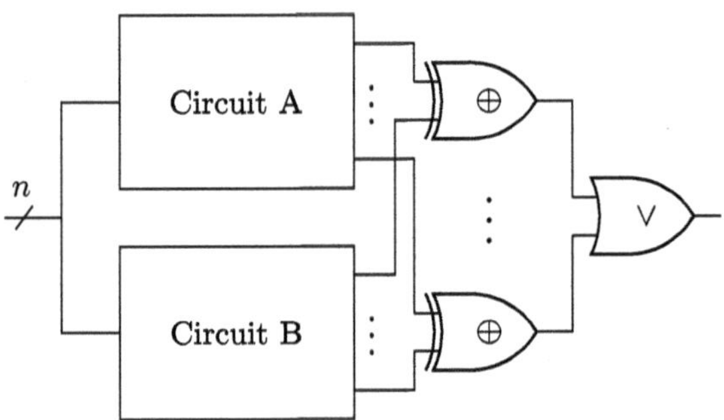

Fig. 2.1 Miter circuit

For the adder function it is well known that it can be represented by a BDD, that has a size that is linear in the number of variables [16]. But in [5] it has been proven that the time and space resources needed for the entire symbolic simulation are polynomially bounded. Hence, this proves that PFV of adders is possible.

In general, this cannot be automatically assumed for any verification method, considering the **complexity of the underlying problems**, as already listed in Chap. 1. But nonetheless, plenty of circuits exist, which can be verified efficiently. The problem is that it is hard to predict for a given circuit, how the resource usage will behave throughout the verification process.

2.2   Approach to a Proof

Compared to the verification of the adder function, often additional adjustments have to be considered, so that PFV can be proven.

2.2.1   Data Structures

Different representations for functions can be compared to reduce the size needed for certain functions. E.g. while the multiplier function is exponential in size when using BDDs, the size grows linearly with respect to the input size if based on a *Multiplicative Binary Moment Diagram* (*BMD) instead [17]. Hence, representations at bit-level and word-level can be interchanged. But next to the size of a data structure, the bounds of the respective algorithms are vital as well. The number of steps needed when applying an operation to BDDs is bounded by the product of the size of both inputs, but for *BMDs no polynomial bound can be given for the number of recursive calls.

2.2.2   Decision Procedure

Further, a variation of the underlying approach can be beneficial as well. E.g., instead of a BDD-based approach a method utilizing SAT can be used. In [6] PFV has been shown for circuits with limited cutwidth based on SAT. Similarly, the PFV based on *Answer Set Programming* (ASP) has been proven in [7] for approximate adders with a constant cutwidth. Since this is a property of the circuit implementation, it is ignored by BDDs, which only represent information about the function computed by a circuit and none about the specific topology.

2.2.3   Divide-and-Conquer

Dividing a complex circuit, that is to be verified, into several parts can be a successful approach. Such a divide-and-conquer strategy has been proposed in [8] to verify non-trivial multiplier circuits. Multipliers consist of three different stages, that can be exchanged or verified separately. This further yields the possibility to combine different formal approaches in a hybrid proof engine, like one acting on bit-level and one for the word-level.

2.2.4 Automatic Proofs

While all options mentioned so far have to be selected and analyzed manually, there has been research on automatically proving PFV as well. In [18] a first step towards this was taken by generating automatic induction proofs for upper bounds for the size of a given BDD.

2.3 Application to Combinational Circuits

A very first example for PFV has been given in 1997 in [19]. There, polynomial upper bounds were proven for the complexity of the *BMD-based verification of Wallace-tree-like multiplier circuits. The idea of guaranteeing the efficient verification of multipliers has now been revived about 20 years later. Based on *Symbolic Computer Algebra* (SCA) it could be extended for a considerably more extensive class of multiplier circuits [8]. Since then PFV could be proven for a range of different circuits, some of them were already mentioned in this thesis.

The verification of floating point adders was addressed in [9]. The intermediate results of the BDD-based symbolic simulation of several examples were analyzed, to extract two main points during the verification, where the BDDs grew exponentially with respect to the number of inputs n. These blow-ups were then prevented based on an adequate case-splitting, where the identified critical parts of the BDD were simplified for each case. The number of cases had to be polynomial with respect to n and together the cases had to completely verify the floating point adder. With the proposed case-splitting BDD-based PFV was proven for floating point adders.

So far examples were given, where the verification of circuits that compute a specific operation or class of functions were considered in an isolated manner. But in [10], PFV was proven for a complete RISC-V processor. All its functional units were covered, which were each divided into different cases, to be verified on their own. E.g. for the unit for decoding and the ALU different functionalities were extracted, to be symbolically simulated separately. This results in cases for each supported instruction, like addition, jumping or shifting. That way, an intermediate blow-up in memory used for the verification is prevented and PFV could be be proven for the entire processor.

2.4   Application to Sequential Circuits

While several successful examples of PFV could be named for combinational circuits in the previous section, the application of the concept to sequential circuits
has barely been explored. The complexity of the verification task is increased by
having to consider the state of a circuit next to the applied inputs. When using the
miter circuit shown in Fig. 2.1 for SEC, it has to, again, evaluate to "0" for every
combination of inputs, but for any sequence of states as well.

The increased complexity can be reduced by turning the sequential problem into
a combinational problem, so that the methods of the previous section are again applicable. This is done during *Bounded Model Checking* (BMC) by unrolling the circuit
for some k steps. A similar approach has been used in the previously mentioned
proof of PFV for a complete processor in [10]. There, it was only referred to the
combinational units of the processor, but the proof also argues about its sequential
control unit. The stages of this unit are simulated for several clock cycles in a row,
to be then compared with a reference. A similar approach could be used when verifying a processor, that has a pipeline. But it is easy to see that this approach can only
be applied, if the entire sequential behavior of the considered circuit is covered by
these k steps for a limited size of k. Otherwise either the verification is not complete
anymore or PFV can not be achieved. Therefore, different concepts are necessary,
for the efficient verification of circuits with a more extensive sequential behavior.

Preliminaries

In this section, an overview over the used concepts is given. This includes a review of the basics needed for BDD-based model checking and for reversible functions. Further, the circuits considered in this thesis are defined.

3.1 Binary Decision Diagrams

Various approaches for a useful representation and manipulation of Boolean functions exist, each with their own advantages and disadvantages. For this thesis, a focus on BDDs has been chosen.

Definition 3.1 *A **Binary Decision Diagram (BDD)** [16] is a directed, acyclic graph. It represents a Boolean function $f : B^n \rightarrow B$ with variables $x_0, x_1, \ldots, x_{n-1}$ by use of the Shannon decomposition*

$$f = \overline{x}_i f|_{\overline{x}_i} + x_i f|_{x_i}$$

*in each internal node. Here, the notation $f|_{x_i}$ denotes that f is being restricted by the assignment $x_i = 1$, which is called the **high child** of the node. Analogously, $f|_{\overline{x}_i}$ denotes the restriction by a negative assignment and is called the **low child**. The two terminal nodes have the constant values "1" and "0".*

Example 3.1 *Two BDDs can be seen in Fig. 3.1(a) and Fig. 3.1(b). The edges for a high child are depicted as solid lines and the edges for a low child as dashed lines.*

C. Dominik, *Embedding Sequential Circuits for their Polynomial Formal Verification*, BestMasters, https://doi.org/10.1007/978-3-658-50155-6_3

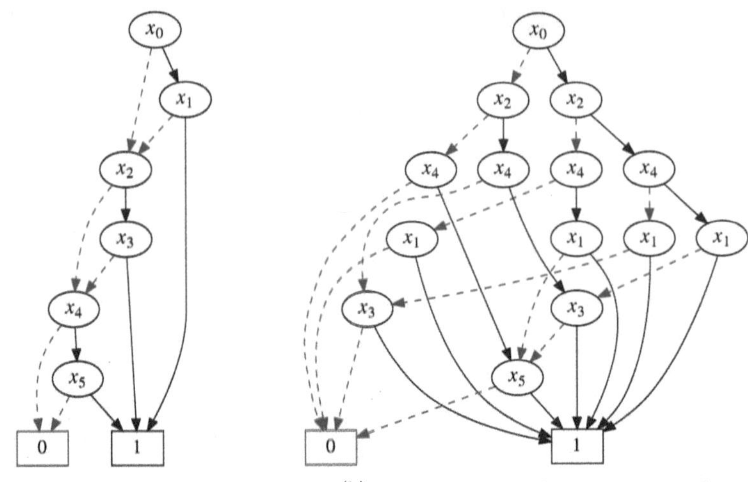

(a) With variable order $(x_0, x_1, x_2, x_3, x_4, x_5)$. (b) With variable order $(x_0, x_2, x_4, x_1, x_3, x_5)$.

Fig. 3.1 BDDs for the function $(x_0 \cdot x_1) + (x_2 \cdot x_3) + (x_4 \cdot x_5)$

The size of a BDD G is denoted by $|G|$ and defined as the number of internal nodes. This size is decreased by using two reduction rules, introduced in the following definition, that eliminate nodes without changing the function which is being represented.

Definition 3.2 *Two distinct nodes in a BDD, that represent the same function, are called **isomorphic subgraphs**. A single node, with an identical high and low child, is called **redundant**. A BDD is called **reduced**, if all isomorphic subgraphs and redundancies are removed.*

Definition 3.3 *A BDD is **ordered** if all variables follow a given variable order* $(x_0, x_1, \ldots x_{n-1})$.

The BDDs considered in this thesis are reduced and ordered. Because of these two properties, BDDs are a canonical form of representation for Boolean functions. This means, two BDDs representing the same function, must be identical. Because of this, it is simple to test BDDs for equivalence. Another advantage is the performance of manipulating BDDs. Applying an operation like the disjunction "$\vee$" or the conjunction "$\wedge$" to two BDDs G and H has a number of required steps limited by $\mathcal{O}(|G| \cdot |H|)$, this bound holds for the result size as well. Often, other operations can be represented based on this. E.g. a restriction $G|_x$ can be written as $G \wedge x$. Because "$\wedge$" is used, this has a runtime in $\mathcal{O}(|G| \cdot |x|)$, which can be reduced to $\mathcal{O}(|G|)$, as the BDD for x is only one node. And the existential quantification $\exists x \, G$ is equivalent to $G|_{\overline{x}_i} \vee G|_{x_i}$, which hence has a runtime in $\mathcal{O}(|G|^2)$. While BDDs are an efficient representation of Boolean functions in many cases, their size can be exponential with respect to n as well. This can be influenced by the chosen variable order, which sometimes drastically decreases the size to be linear in n.

Example 3.2 *In [16] a function based on n pairs is introduced to illustrate the effect a different variable order can have on the size of a BDD. It is defined as*

$$(x_0 \cdot x_1) + (x_2 \cdot x_3) + \cdots + (x_{2n-2} \cdot x_{2n-1}).$$

With an increasing variable order $(x_0, x_1, \ldots, x_{2n-1})$, the BDD representing this function has $2 \cdot n$ nodes. This can be seen for $n = 3$ in Fig. 3.1(a). But with a variable order $(x_0, x_2, x_4, \ldots, x_{2n-2}, x_1, x_3, \ldots, x_{2n-1})$, $2^{n+1} - 2$ nodes are necessary. The corresponding BDD with $n = 3$ is shown in Fig. 3.1(b). Hence, for this example the variable order can decide between a linear and an exponential increase in the number of nodes.

3.2   Symbolic Model Checking

A well-established method for the formal verification of the temporal properties of systems is model checking (see Chapter 1 of [4]). The system is modeled by a state-transition graph and analyzed with automated formal methods. A way to define the graph is with a FSM.

Definition 3.4 *A FSM can be formalized by the triple $\langle Q, I, T \rangle$. The set of m states $Q = \{q_0, q_1, \ldots, q_{m-1}\}$ is represented by the vertices of the graph. The states in the set $I \subseteq Q$ are the initial states. The edges between the states are given by the transition relation $T \subseteq Q \times Q$.*

Example 3.3 *The FSM of a 3-bit full counter (defined in the following Sect. 3.3) can be seen in Fig. 3.2.*

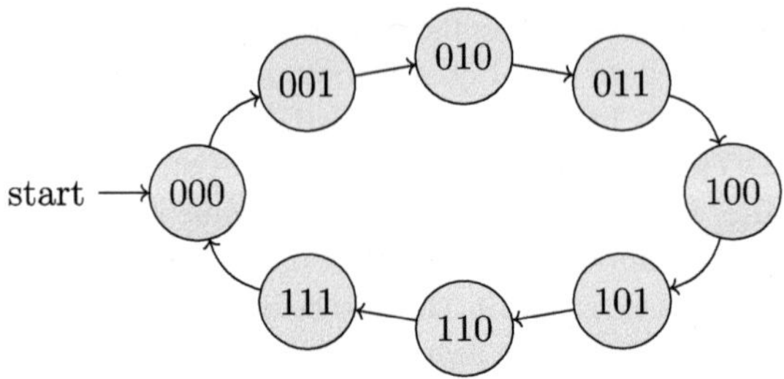

Fig. 3.2 FSM of a 3-bit full counter

When considering realistic examples, a symbolic representation, of the transition relation T and any set of states is necessary, to handle the state space which the model has to cover (see Chapter 8 of [4]). This representation can e.g. be based on BDDs. Such a method is called SMC.

A fundamental step when analyzing the behavior of a system, is to identify which states are reachable starting from the initial states, which is done by SRA. The corresponding algorithm can be seen in Fig. 3.3. It starts with an empty set of reachable states Q_r, which is filled throughout the algorithm and returned at the end. The frontier set F contains all states, which are reachable within one step. Therefore, it is initially set to an initial state $q_0 \in I$. Both sets are repeatedly updated until the frontier set is empty. For this, Q_r is extended by the current state of F and the new frontier F is set to all states resulting from an image computation, that have not been reached yet. The image calculates all successors of F with

$$image(F, T) := rename(\exists S(F \wedge T)).$$

1: $Q_r := \emptyset$ ▷ Set of reachable states
2: $F := q_0$ ▷ Frontier set
3: **repeat**
4:     $Q_r := Q_r \vee F$
5:     $F := image(F, T) \wedge \overline{Q_r}$
6: **until** $F = \emptyset$
7: **return** Q_r

Fig. 3.3 Algorithm for SMC

With $F \wedge T$ all transitions starting with a state in F are selected, which includes current states and successor states. A current state over n bits consists of the current state variables $S = \{s_0, \ldots, s_{n-1}\}$ and a successor state of the successor state variables $S' = \{s'_0, \ldots, s'_{n-1}\}$. The current state variables are removed from the resulting transitions with $\exists S(F \wedge T)$, which denotes a recursive application of $\exists s_i(\exists S(F \wedge T))$ for all s_i in S until $S = \emptyset$. The s_i are removed starting with s_0 and going to s_{n-1}. Finally, each s'_i is exchanged with the equivalent s_i using $rename$. The maximum number of steps is exactly the number of reachable states of the FSM, but the operations "$\wedge$" and "$\exists$" in $image$ can have intermediate results of severely bigger size compared to the inputs. Hence, this step forms the bottleneck of the algorithm. For further analysis of the system, the properties which hold in the states in Q_r are examined.

3.3   Counter Circuits

As a case study, counter circuits are used in this thesis, which are defined in the following. For this a general understanding of circuits is assumed, including e.g. flip-flops.

Definition 3.5 *A **full n-bit counter** (FC_n) has n flip-flops $ff_0, ff_1, \ldots, ff_{n-1}$. The flip-flops are all set to "0" in the beginning and count up in binary with each clock signal. After taking the final value "$2^n - 1$", all flip-flops are reset to "0".*

The behavior of such a full n-bit counter can be visualized by a FSM. For this, the flip-flops of the circuit have to be encoded using states of the FSM. This is easiest done with a binary encoding: Let state q be a state in the FSM and s_i the i-th variable of q. Then the state q encodes the circuit with $s_i := ff_i$.

Example 3.4 *The FSM for a full n-bit counter with $n = 3$ is visualized in Fig. 3.2.*

Definition 3.6 *An **n-bit modulo-m counter** "$M_m C_n$" counts in a similar manner as in Definition 3.5. But here the final value before the reset is $m - 1$ with $0 < m \le 2^n$.*

Example 3.5 *The FSM for an n-bit modulo-6 counter with $n = 3$ and $m = 6$ is visualized in Fig. 3.4.*

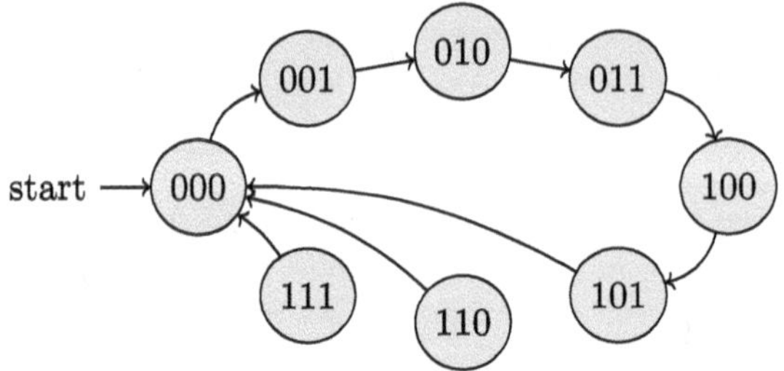

Fig. 3.4 FSM of a 3-bit modulo-6 counter

3.4   Reversible Boolean Functions

A class of Boolean functions, which is considered in this thesis, are functions that can be reversed. Not only can each output be derived based on a given input, but the same holds for the opposite direction. To define this class, first another definition is necessary.

Definition 3.7 *A function is called **injective**, if no two values of the domain are mapped to the same value of the co-domain. A function is called **surjective**, if each value of the co-domain is mapped to at least once. If a function is both injective and surjective, it is called **bijective**.*

Definition 3.8 *A **reversible function** (see Chapter 2 of [12]) is a Boolean function $f : B^n \rightarrow B^n$, for which the following two conditions hold:*

1. *It has an equal number of inputs and outputs n.*
2. *It is bijective, thus computes a permutation of these n inputs.*

Example 3.6 *A simple example for a reversible function is the negation $f(x) = \overline{x}$. Additional examples can be found in Table 3.1:*

- *The truth table for the logical conjunction "$\wedge$" can be seen in Table 3.1(a). It is easy to see that this function does not fulfill either of the two conditions for a reversible function. It has two inputs but only one output and an input value cannot distinctively be derived, if the output value is "0". But every value of*

Table 3.1 Truth tables for conjunction "$y = x_0 \wedge x_1$"

(a) Conjunction "$\wedge$".

x_0	x_1	y
0	0	0
0	1	0
1	0	0
1	1	1

(b) With garbage outputs.

x_0	x_1	y	g_0	g_1
0	0	0	0	0
0	1	0	0	1
1	0	0	1	0
1	1	1	1	1

(c) With constant input.

c_0	x_0	x_1	y	g_0	g_1
0	0	0	0	0	0
0	0	1	0	0	1
0	1	0	0	1	0
0	1	1	1	1	1
1	0	0	0	1	1
1	0	1	1	0	0
1	1	0	1	0	1
1	1	1	1	1	0

the co-domain $B^1 = \{0, 1\}$ is mapped to at least once, hence the function is surjective.

- *The function depicted in Table 3.1(c) on the other hand has three inputs and three outputs and every value in the co-domain B^3 is mapped to, but only once. Hence, this function is reversible.*

A noteworthy detail is that not every bijective function must be reversible as well. E.g. the function shown in Table 3.1(b) is bijective, if the co-domain is not defined as B^3, but as the four output assignments seen in the truth table. Then only the first condition for a reversible function is not met.

Definition 3.9 *A circuit, which computes a reversible function, is called a **reversible circuit**.*

3.5 Embedding

Most functions are not reversible ones, as described in the last section. This is even the case for very common examples, like the conjunction "$\wedge$" discussed in Example 3.6. Whenever such an irreversible function is needed in the context of reversible functions, it has to be modified accordingly.

Definition 3.10 *An irreversible function* $f : B^n \rightarrow B^m$ *can be turned into a reversible one by* **embedding** *it (see Chapter 2 and 3 of [12]). For this, f has to be altered, so that the two conditions of Definition 3.8 hold. This is done with the following steps, commonly applied in that order:*

1. *The second property is met by adding k outputs to f so that it becomes bijective. Their value is irrelevant for the correct definition of the function and they are not used after the function has been computed. Therefore, these outputs are called* **garbage outputs**.
2. *For the first property, c inputs are added until $n + c = m + k$. They can each be set to any value, as they, analogously, do not influence the function definition. Because of this, they cannot be connected to any other component in the context of a system, which is why they are called* **constant inputs**.

The resulting function $e(f) : B^{n+c} \rightarrow B^{m+k}$ *embeds f.*

Example 3.7 *The truth table for the function* $y = x_0 \wedge x_1$ *is shown in Table 3.1(a). For one possible embedding of this function, the following two steps are applied:*

1. *Two garbage outputs g_0 and g_1, that copy the input values, are added. The result can be seen in Table 3.1(b), the function is now injective.*
2. *A constant input is added in Table 3.1(c). It is set to "0" for all output values of the previous step and to "1" for all remaining output patterns of B^3. The final function is reversible.*

The previous example only shows one possible embedding for the considered function. There, the simple option is chosen, to add n garbage outputs, which copy the value of all input variables. It is easy to find other possible variants. As shown in [20], the minimal number of garbage outputs can be calculated based on the maximum number of repetitions M of any of the output patterns. At least $\lceil log_2(M) \rceil$ garbage outputs are required.

Example 3.8 *Considering the conjunction "$\wedge$" of Example 3.7, the output pattern "0" is the pattern, that is repeated the most times with $M = 3$. Since $\lceil log_2(3) \rceil = 2$, it is not possible to find another embedding with less than the two added garbage outputs of the example.*

This gives the minimal number of additional outputs and in this way the minimal number of constant inputs as well. But their specific embedding, meaning an assignment, which ensures the bijectivity of the function, is not implied by this. Finding such an assignment for the added inputs and outputs without exceeding this minimum is challenging. It is called an **optimal embedding** and calculating it has been proven to be coNP-hard in [21], even if parameters of the embedding problem are restricted. Therefore, heuristic algorithms are necessary for larger functions, because the explicit embedding based on the truth table of the function is not feasible then.

This thesis focuses on BDD-based approaches, of which one for determining M is proposed in [21]. It starts with the BDD for an irreversible function $f : B^n \rightarrow B^m$, which is ordered according to the variable order $(y_0, \ldots, y_{m-1}, x_0, \ldots, x_{n-1})$. That way, the input patterns are sorted above the output patterns. Now a set V of all nodes x_i with $0 \leq i < n - 1$, which are the immediate child of some node y_j with $0 \leq j < m - 1$, is analyzed. These nodes in V each have exactly one incoming edge. This previous path therefore relates each node with exactly one output pattern. The subgraph of each node in V describes a set of input patterns, combined all sets form a partition of the domain B^n. Hence, M can be computed by counting the number of input patterns each node in V represents and comparing them, to find the maximum.

Example 3.9 *The BDD for an irreversible function can be seen in Fig. 3.5. As described, the variables are ordered as $(y_0, y_1, y_2, x_0, x_1, x_2)$. All nodes of x_i in V are colored in gray, as described each only has one incoming edge. Counting their outgoing paths, each node is followed by exactly one input pattern, except for the last one, as seen from left to right. The subgraph of this last x_i-node describes the three input patterns "110" and "101" and "111". Therefore, $M = 3$ must hold. Since this x_i-node is preceeded by the path representing the output pattern "000", these three input patterns all are mapped to this output pattern.*

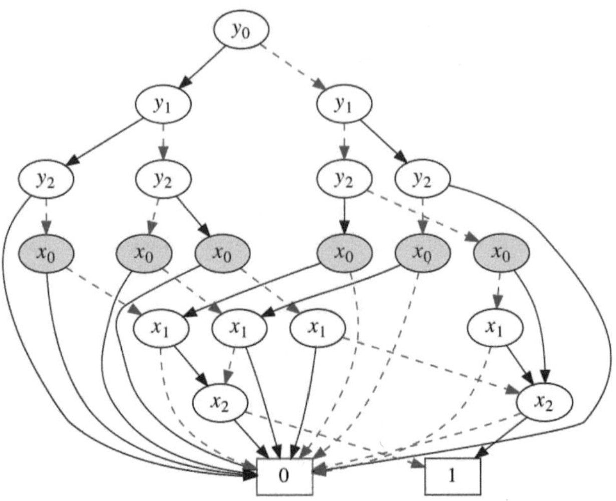

Fig. 3.5 BDD for an irreversible function

Another BDD-based method is proposed in [21], that constructs an embedding for an irreversible function $f : B^n \rightarrow B^m$, but it is heuristic. The corresponding embedded $h(f) : B^{n+m} \rightarrow B^{n+m}$ is constructed as a BDD based on the Bennett Embedding proposed in[22]. This method adds n garbage outputs, of which each g_i with $0 \leq i < n$ is defined as $g_i := x_i$. Further, m constant inputs are added. For each input pattern $x_0 \ldots x_{n-1}$ taken from f, any constant c_j with $0 \leq j < m$ is set to "0", if the corresponding y_j in $h(f)$ is similar to the value it had in f, which is $f_j(x_0, \ldots, x_{n-1})$. Otherwise it is set to "1". Hence $y_j := c_j \oplus f_j(x_0, \ldots, x_{n-1})$.

Verification of Full Counter Circuits

In this section, the verification of full counters is viewed as a first case study on the PFV of sequential circuits. A model checking variant aimed to decrease the resource demands is introduced and then applied to full counters. This application is analyzed with respect to the required resources.

Let us consider an n-bit full counter, given as the BDD T for the transition relation of a FSM. The FSM for $n = 3$ can be seen in Fig. 3.2. Now, the algorithm for SMC, as described in Sect. 3.2, has to be analyzed with respect to PFV. A significant difficulty can easily be seen: The FSM has 2^n states, which the algorithm adds to Q_r one step at a time. Consequently, the algorithm must execute 2^n steps, to cover the entire FSM. This property of the circuit is called an **exponential sequential depth** and seems to make the application within polynomial resources impossible. For other circuits it is an option, to alter certain aspects of the verification process, e.g. choose a specific implementation of the circuit, optimize the variable order or encoding of states in a BDD or use another representation format altogether. This could minimize the required resources and, by this means, reduce an exponential runtime to a polynomial one. But in the case of a full counter, all of these options are bound to be unsuccessful, because they cannot affect the underlying procedure of the SMC-algorithm. Therefore, an alternative variant of the model checking algorithm is needed to overcome this difficulty. Such a variant is described in the following.

4.1   Restricted Domain Model Checking

To make PFV for circuits with an exponential sequential depth possible, the algorithm for SMC has to be modified. This variant is called Restricted Domain Model Checking (RDMC) [11] and alters the following four aspects:

© The Author(s), under exclusive license to Springer Fachmedien Wiesbaden GmbH, part of Springer Nature 2026

C. Dominik, *Embedding Sequential Circuits for their Polynomial Formal Verification*, BestMasters, https://doi.org/10.1007/978-3-658-50155-6_4

1. **Number of initial states**: SMC starts with a single initial state q_0, e.g. all state variables set to "0" for a full counter. RDMC instead starts with sets of initial states. These sets are obtained from the domain of the given FSM, which are the current state variables S. Each state variable s_i is restricted with $s_i := 0$, which gives the initial set $S_{\bar{s}_i}$. Analogously, each variable is restricted with $s_i := 1$ for the initial set S_{s_i}. The set of all $2 \cdot n$ initial sets is called $\mathbb{I}$.

2. **Number of executions**: The algorithm for SMC is executed a single time. Meanwhile, RDMC executes the algorithm for each initial set $I \in \mathbb{I}$. For an FSM with n state bits this is $2 \cdot n$ times.

3. **Depth of execution**: The SMC-algorithm is exhaustively executed until the frontier set F contains no further states. Considering the example of the full counter, this can result in up to 2^n steps. RDMC on the other hand only executes the algorithm for one step.

4. **Return value**: Whereas SMC returns a set of reachable states Q_r, RDMC returns a set $\mathbb{Q}_r$, that contains $2 \cdot n$ sets. Any state q in B^n can be represented by the intersection of n sets in $\mathbb{I}$ by restricting each state variable s_i exactly once to either "0" or "1". In a similar way, the successor of q can be computed with the intersection of the same n sets, but after $image(I, T)$ has been applied to them. This way, the resulting sets in $\mathbb{Q}_r$ ensure the correct behavior of the circuit in the same way the result of the algorithm for SMC does.

The algorithm for RDMC can be seen in Fig. 4.1, to be compared to the SMC-algorithm in Fig. 3.3.

```
1:  S := {s_0, s_1, ..., s_{n-1}}                    ▷ Set of state variables
2:  Q_r := ∅
3:  for s_i ∈ S do
4:      S_{s̄_i} := (S ∧ s̄_i)              ▷ Restrict state variables with s_i := 0
5:      S_{s_i} := (S ∧ s_i)               ▷ Restrict state variables with s_i := 1
6:      Q_r.append(image(S_{s̄_i}, T))
7:      Q_r.append(image(S_{s_i}, T))
8:  end for
9:  return Q_r
```

Fig. 4.1 Algorithm for RDMC

Table 4.1 Sets computed during RDMC of a 3-bit full counter.

s_i	$I \in \mathbb{I}$	$image(I, T)$
$\overline{s}_2$	$\{0,1,\mathbf{2},3\}$	$\{\mathbf{1,2,3,4}\}$
s_2	$\{4,5,6,7\}$	$\{5,6,7,0\}$
$\overline{s}_1$	$\{0,1,4,5\}$	$\{1,2,5,6\}$
s_1	$\{\mathbf{2},3,6,7\}$	$\{\mathbf{3,4,7,0}\}$
$\overline{s}_0$	$\{0,\mathbf{2},4,6\}$	$\{\mathbf{1,3,5,7}\}$
s_0	$\{1,3,5,7\}$	$\{2,4,6,0\}$

Example 4.1 *The calculations of RDMC for a 3-bit full counter can be seen in Table 4.1. As described in Step 1 of the algorithm, the first column shows which s_i is restricted to result in the initial sets in $\mathbb{I}$ seen in the second column. The corresponding resulting sets described in Step 4 can be found in the third column.*

The state "$2 = 0b010$" can be written as the intersection of the initial sets $S|_{\overline{s}_2}$, $S|_{s_1}$ and $S|_{\overline{s}_0}$ as marked in bold in the second column. To further illustrate this, these sets are highlighted in the FSM of a 3-bit full counter in Fig. 4.3(a). Set $S|_{\overline{s}_2}$ is marked by diagonal lines, set $S|_{s_1}$ by dots and set $S|_{\overline{s}_0}$ by horizontal lines. The only state, where they all overlap, is state "010", which is marked in bold.

The corresponding resulting sets of the execution for each initial set are marked in bold in the third column of Table 4.1. As expected, their intersection $\{1, 2, 3, 4\} \cap \{3, 4, 7, 0\} \cap \{1, 3, 5, 7\}$ only includes the successor state "3". Again, these sets are highlighted in a FSM in Fig. 4.2(b). Each resulting set is marked by the pattern used for the corresponding initial set in Fig. 4.2(a). State "011", where all resulting sets

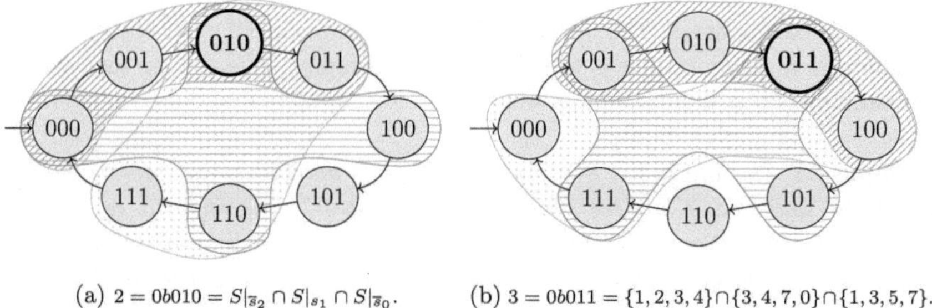

(a) $2 = 0b010 = S|_{\overline{s}_2} \cap S|_{s_1} \cap S|_{\overline{s}_0}$.   (b) $3 = 0b011 = \{1,2,3,4\} \cap \{3,4,7,0\} \cap \{1,3,5,7\}$.

Fig. 4.2 FSMs of a 3-bit full counter with intersecting sets of states that give state "2" and its successor

intersect, is marked in bold. Overall, the six rows of Table 4.1 depict the $2 \cdot n = 6$ executions of the algorithm, as stated in Step 2 of the algorithm.

Example 4.2 *Analogously to Example 4.1, state "$4 = 0b100$" can be written as the intersection of the initial sets $S|_{s_2}$, $S|_{\overline{s}_1}$ and $S|_{\overline{s}_0}$, as illustrated by gray underlines in Table 4.1. The sets are further highlighted by diagonal lines, by dots and by horizontal lines, respectively, in the FSM of a 3-bit full counter in Fig. 4.3(a). They all overlap in state "100", which is marked in bold.*

The corresponding resulting sets of the execution per initial set are underlined in gray in Table 4.1 and highlighted in a FSM in Fig. 4.3(a) by the pattern of the corresponding initial set in Fig. 4.3(b). Their intersection only includes the successor state "$5 = 101$" that is marked in bold.

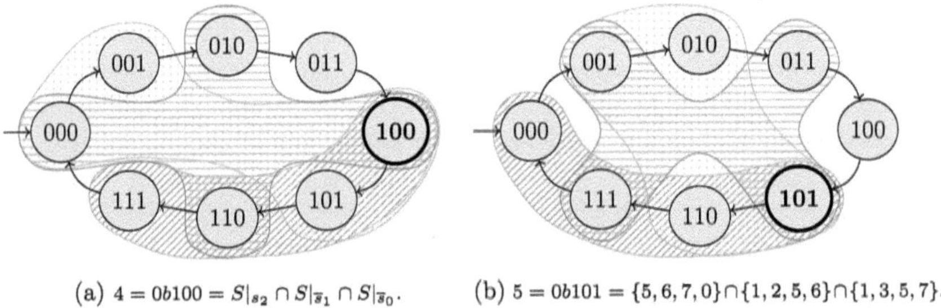

(a) $4 = 0b100 = S|_{s_2} \cap S|_{\overline{s}_1} \cap S|_{\overline{s}_0}$.   (b) $5 = 0b101 = \{5,6,7,0\} \cap \{1,2,5,6\} \cap \{1,3,5,7\}$.

Fig. 4.3 FSMs of a 3-bit full counter with intersecting sets of states that give state "4" and its successor

Based on these first applications of RDMC, the approach of this model checking variant can be examined. The method analyzes the behavior of each of the n state variables of the circuit, that is to be verified, separately. This can be seen when comparing e.g. Fig. 4.2(a) and Fig. 4.2(b).

Example 4.3 *The initial set $S|_{\overline{s}_2} = \{0, 1, 2, 3\}$ is marked by diagonal lines in Fig. 4.2(a) and selects half the states of the domain B^n. The opposite restriction $S|_{s_2}$ would select the other half of B^n. The co-domain B^n is split in half in a similar way by these restrictions, as can be seen in Fig. 4.2(b). The resulting set $image(S|_{\overline{s}_2}, T)$ is marked by diagonal lines, the remaining states form the resulting set $image(S|_{s_2}, T)$. Together, both sets therefore represent the effect, which flipping the variable s_2 has on the co-domain.*

This example illustrates that a pair of resulting sets $image(S|_{\overline{s_i}}, T)$ and $image(S|_{s_i}, T)$ describes the **influence of a variable s_i on the co-domain** of a function. The set $\mathbb{Q}_r$ of all resulting sets then describes the influence of all of the variables. Compared to this SMC analyzes the influence of a specific state or set of states. Further, RDMC defines the behavior of a circuit in an even more specific way. Whereas the result Q_r of SMC only declares, which states are reachable in general, the result $\mathbb{Q}_r$ of RDMC further contains the information about the specific transitions between all states.

It is stated in Step 4 of the algorithm that the successor of any state q can be computed based on the results of RDMC. This statement is not accurate for every function, because it is possible that the result of the intersection contains more states than the desired state. For RDMC to be applicable, the result when computing the successor for any state has to be distinctive. This is the case if the following equation holds:

$$\forall q \in B^n : \bigcap_{\{I \mid I \in \mathbb{I} \wedge q \in I\}} image(I, T) = \{image(q, T)\}.$$

It is easy to see that this equation holds for any bijective function. The left part of the equation distinctively defines a single current state, hence the right part must as well. Therefore this equation holds for any full counter.

4.2 Polynomial Upper Bounds

We now apply RDMC to full counters and prove that based on this method PFV is possible. As explained in Sect. 3.2, the bottleneck of the SMC-algorithm are the operations "$\wedge$" and "$\exists$". This is also the case for RDMC. Therefore, to prove polynomial upper bounds the BDDs, to which these operations are applied, have to be analyzed. It is evident that each set I can be represented by a BDD of one node. The size of the transition relation T has to be in $\mathcal{O}(n^2)$. The following Lemma considering this has been proven in [11] (see Lemma III.1). For a self-contained thesis, the proof is given here again.

Lemma 4.1 *Let BDD T describe the transition relation of a full n-bit counter with the pair-wise variable order $(s_0, s_0', s_1, s_1', \ldots, s_{n-1}, s_{n-1}')$. Then $|T| \leq 5 \cdot n$ holds.*

Proof. Due to the variable order, the BDD T traverses a current state q from the Least Significant Bit (LSB) s_0 to the Most Significant Bit (MSB) s_{n-1}. Based on this, the effect, which the process of counting up has on the variables in q, can be divided into two phases, which are both represented by different components in T:

1. **The value is flipped**: The counting affects the variables, while q is in this phase. This means, the value of a successor state variable s_i' is set to the opposite value of the corresponding current state variable s_i. As long as q stays in this phase, any value is flipped from "1" to "0", which is described by the component $s_i \overline{s_i'}$. The phase ends with a final variable being flipped from "0" to "1", given by the component $\overline{s_i} s_i'$. If the phase does not end with the final variable, Phase 2 is entered by this.

2. **The value is kept**: Now, the counting has no effect on the variables of q anymore. Any s_i' is set to exactly the same value, which the corresponding s_i has. This is described by the component $s_i s_i' + \overline{s_i}\,\overline{s_i'}$.

This analysis shows that the variables of a pair (s_i, s_i') strongly depend on each other, hence a pair-wise variable order is beneficial. But the phases further show that each pair depends on the phase of the previous pair as well. To represent this behavior, the described components need at most two nodes for Phase 1 and at most three nodes for Phase 2 per pair of variables (s_i, s_i'). Combined with the number of variables n, the number of nodes in T cannot exceed $5 \cdot n$. $\square$

Example 4.4 *The BDD of an n-bit full counter with $n = 3$ can be seen in Fig. 4.4. The components described in the proof of Lemma 4.1 are marked for the variable pair (s_1, s_1'). The two nodes of Phase 1 can be seen in the right box. This also includes the transition component to the left box, which contains the three nodes of Phase 2. Due to reductions, the phases are less clear for the other two pairs of variables. Further, the BDD has 12 nodes, which is less than $5 \cdot 3 = 15$ and hence underlines the statement of Lemma 4.1.*

Example 4.5 *Compared to Example 4.4, the BDD of an n-bit full counter with $n = 3$ and no variable reodering can be seen in Fig. 4.5. Even for such a small n the effect is evident, as the 12 nodes of a pair-wise variable order are exceeded by 9 nodes.*

Further, the repeated application of "$\exists$" should not increase the BDD size. A demonstration, why this is not automatically the case, is given by the following example.

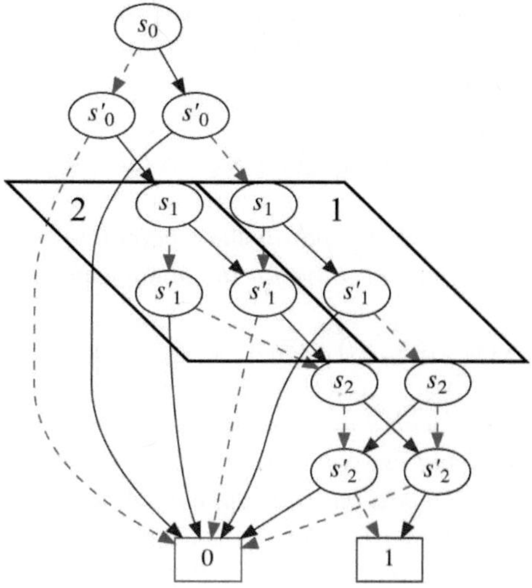

Fig. 4.4 Transition relation of a 3-bit full counter with pair-wise variable order

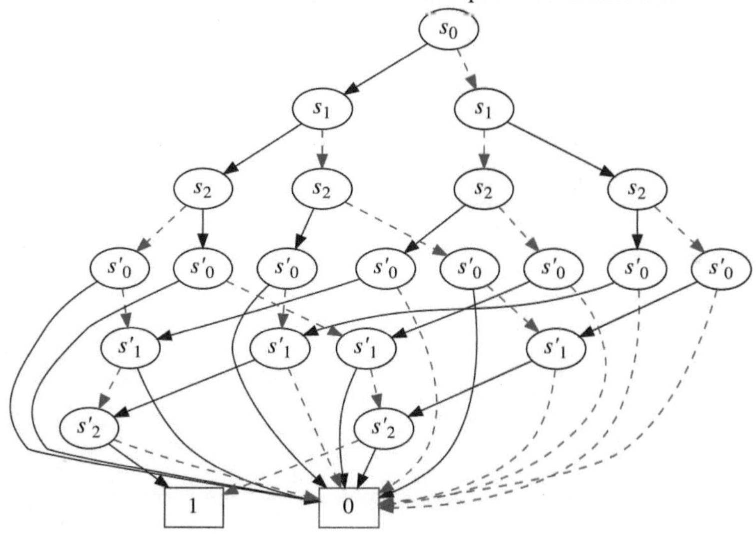

Fig. 4.5 Transition relation of a 3-bit full counter with no reordering

Example 4.6 *Similar to the function discussed in Example 3.2, an "XOR-counterexample" can be constructed by exchanging the "$\wedge$" by "$\oplus$". The function of $2 \cdot n$ variables is then given by*

$$(s_1 \oplus s_1') \wedge (s_2 \oplus s_2') \wedge \cdots \wedge (s_n \oplus s_n').$$

Further, a variable s_0 is added, to separate the n pairs into two halfs. This variable is positive for the first half and negative for the other, which gives

$$(s_0 \wedge (s_1 \oplus s_1') \wedge \cdots \wedge (s_{n/2} \oplus s_{n/2}')) \wedge (\overline{s}_0 \wedge (s_{(n/2)+1} \oplus s_{(n/2)+1}') \wedge \cdots \wedge (s_n \oplus s_n')).$$

The BDD for this function with $n = 2$ can be seen in Fig. 4.6(a). The BDD for the same function after applying $\exists s_0$ can be seen in Fig. 4.6(b). Even for such a small n, this only removes one s_0-node, but adds three nodes for the remaining variables. This is, because the variables are ordered in such a way that depending variables are interlocked with other, independent ones. But the s_0-node still separates these interlocked variables. The effect is more severe for bigger n, which can be seen in Fig. 4.7 and Fig. 4.8 for $n = 3$ and in Fig. 4.9 and Fig. 4.10 for $n = 4$.

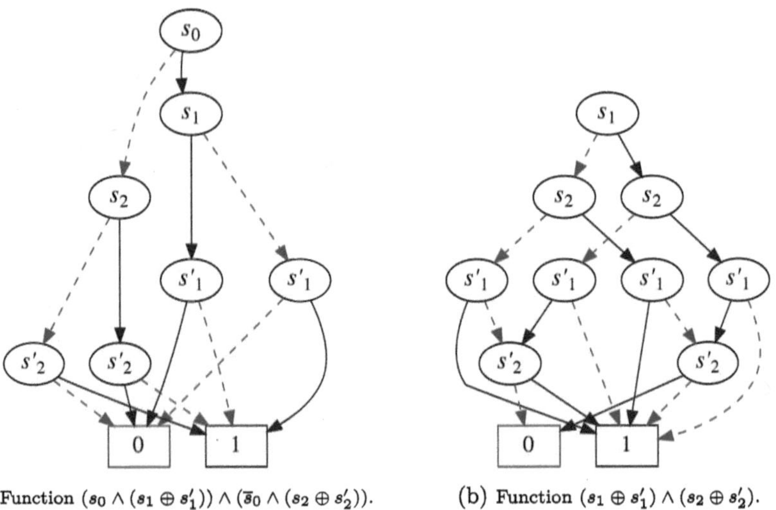

(a) Function $(s_0 \wedge (s_1 \oplus s_1')) \wedge (\overline{s}_0 \wedge (s_2 \oplus s_2'))$.　　　(b) Function $(s_1 \oplus s_1') \wedge (s_2 \oplus s_2')$.

Fig. 4.6 BDDs for XOR-counterexample

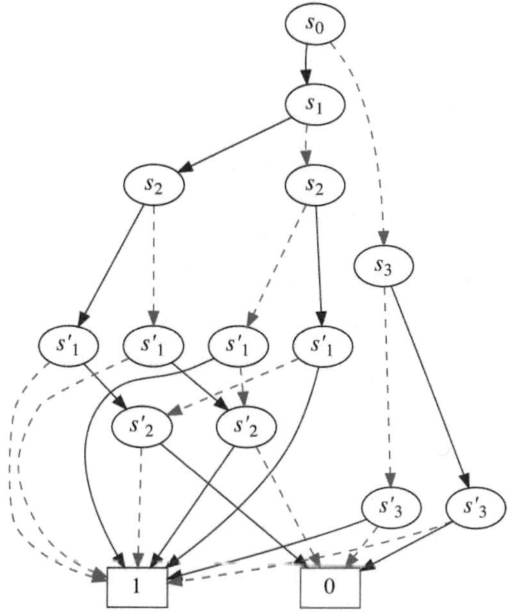

Fig. 4.7 XOR-counterexample for $n = 3$

The following theorem (Theorem III.2 in [11]) proves that such a blow-up caused by the "∃"-operation cannot appear for a full counter. The proof of the theorem further includes a more detailed analysis of the runtime of each step of the algorithm as well.

Theorem 4.1 The time and space demands of RDMC of a full n-bit counter with variables ordered as pairs are in $\mathcal{O}(n^2)$ and $\mathcal{O}(n)$, respectively.

Proof. The algorithm for RDMC, as described in Sect. 4.1, has to be analyzed. For this, each step of the operation $image(I, T)$ is inspected with respect to the full counter's transition relation T:

1. **Conjunction $I \wedge T$:** As stated in Sect. 3.1, the runtime and size of the result for "$\wedge$" are in $\mathcal{O}(|I| \cdot |T|)$. Since I is created by restricting a single variable, the corresponding BDD consists always of exactly one node. Hence, the runtime and size of the result of this step must be in $\mathcal{O}(|T|)$.

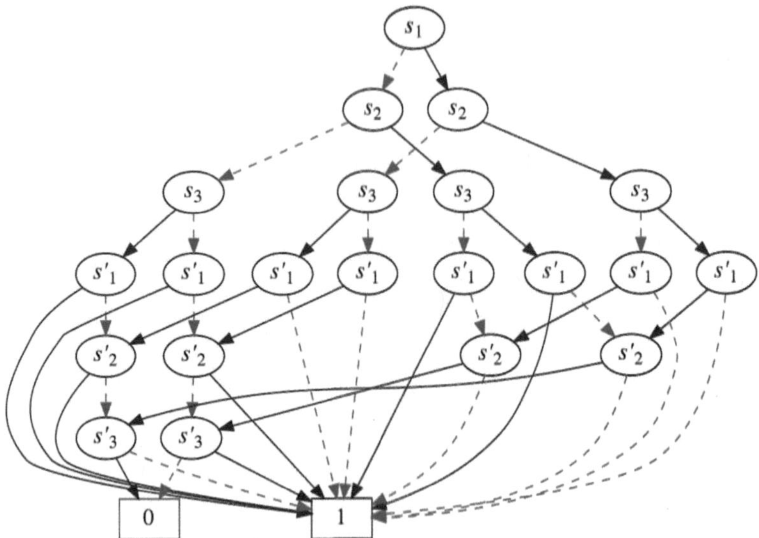

Fig. 4.8 XOR-counterexample for $n = 3$ after $\exists x_0$

2. **Quantification $\exists S$:** Applying $\exists s_i$ to a BDD G can be rewritten as $G|_{\overline{s}_i} \vee G|_{s_i}$, as stated in Sect. 3.1. The first quantification must therefore be in $\mathcal{O}(|T|^2)$, because it is applied to the result of Step 1, which has a size in $\mathcal{O}(|T|)$. The crucial part of this proof is the repeated application of this for all s_i in S. If the result size of all n quantifications is the product of the size of both inputs, the exponent in the runtime would increase dramatically. **This blow-up does not occur, if the result of each quantification has a size smaller or equal to $|T|$.** Then each application would be in $\mathcal{O}(|T|^2)$.

    The nodes in S are quantified going from s_0 to s_{n-1}, this means in a top-down order. The result of Step 1 represents a subset of the transitions in T, hence it consists of the components described in the proof of Lemma 4.1. This also includes components $s_i s_i'$ and $\overline{s}_i \overline{s}_i'$, because component $s_i s_i' + \overline{s}_i \overline{s}_i'$ can be split up during Step 1, if only one of the parts is in the respective subset of T. The effect of the quantification can be analyzed for each case:

    (a) **Component $s_i s_i' + \overline{s}_i \overline{s}_i'$** results in $\overline{s}_i' + s_i'$. This is reduced, because it is redundant.

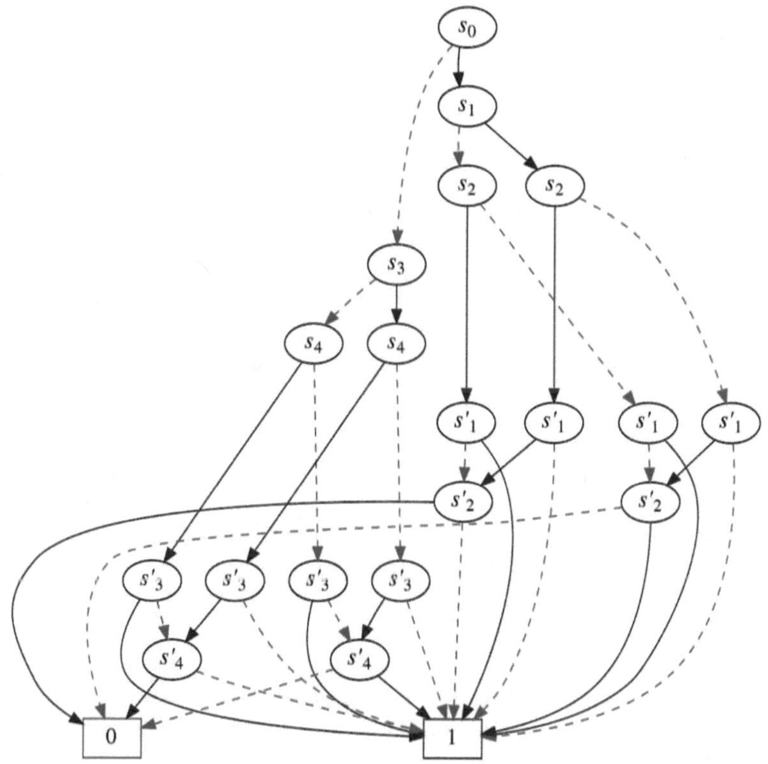

Fig. 4.9 XOR-counterexample for $n = 4$

(b) **Components $\overline{s}_i s_i'$ and $s_i s_i'$** result in s_i'. Hence, the incoming edge of the s_i-node is redirected to the s_i'-node.

(c) **Components $\overline{s}_i \overline{s}_i'$ and $s_i \overline{s}_i'$** result in $\overline{s}_i'$. The incoming edge of the s_i-node is again redirected.

This analysis shows that the number of s_i'-nodes is reduced or equal after each $\exists s_i$. Any variable pair (s_i, s_i') depends only on each other and the phase of the previous pair. The quantification therefore has no effect on the nodes of the following variable pairs. Hence, the argumentation holds for each quantification, which means no new nodes can be created during the overall application of $\exists S$.

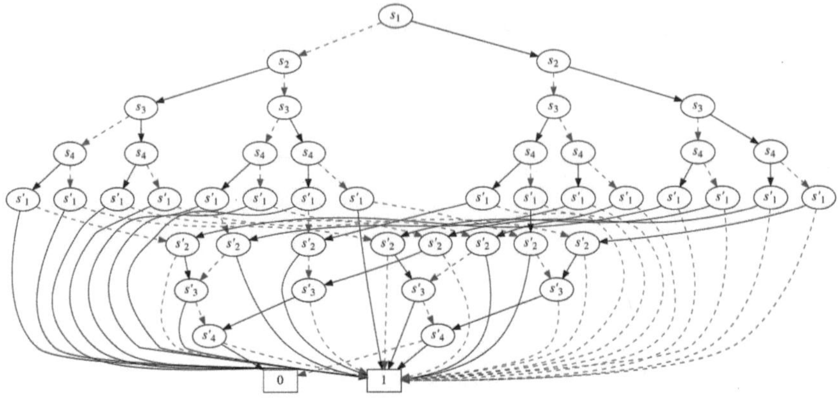

Fig. 4.10 XOR-counterexample for $n = 4$ after $\exists x_0$

3. **Substitution *rename*:** For the simultaneous substitution, the result of Step 2 is traversed and meanwhile the resulting BDD with renamed nodes is built. For this, instead of each s_i'-node, the according s_i-node is used. The number of steps must be in $\mathcal{O}(|T|)$.

This operation $image(I, T)$ is executed for each set $I \in \mathbb{I}$, hence $2 \cdot n$ times. As shown, each step has a runtime in $\mathcal{O}(|T|^2)$ and therefore RDMC must be executable with a number of steps in $\mathcal{O}(|T|^2)$ as well.

Each BDD, which is created during RDMC, is in $\mathcal{O}(|T|)$. The BDD T is needed for the entire process and each of the $2 \cdot n$ executions stores one final result. Further, each execution uses at most three additional BDDs simultaneously during Step 2. The overall space demands are therefore in $\mathcal{O}(|T|)$. Combining this with Lemma 4.1, the time and space resources needed are in $\mathcal{O}(n^2)$ and $\mathcal{O}(n)$. $\square$

With this theorem, the PFV of a full counter circuit has been proven to be possible based on RDMC.

Verification of Modulo Counter Circuits 5

The previous Chap. 4 focused on accelerating the verification of circuits with an exponential sequential depth for bijective functions by considering the example of full counters. However, the computations of modulo counters, as described in Sect. 3.3, often have a similar sequential depth but are not bijective. The model checking variant RDMC, as introduced in Sect. 4.1, can therefore not directly be applied to modulo counters to reduce the exponential runtime when SMC is applied to them. The reason for this is that RDMC does not always have distinctive results for functions that are not bijective. This issue will be illustrated in the following example.

Example 5.1 *The application of RDMC to a 3-bit mod-6 counter is shown in Table 5.1. Similar to Example 4.1 and Example 4.2, the six rows depict the six executions of the algorithm. The first column gives the state bit s_i, which is restricted during each execution, and each set of initial states resulting from this restriction is*

Table 5.1 Sets computed during RDMC of counter circuits

s_i	$I \in \mathbb{I}$	$image(I, T)$		
		$M_6 C_3$	$he(M_6 C_3)$	Modified $F C_3$
$\bar{s}_2$	$\{0,1,2,3\}$	$\{1,2,3,4\}$	$\{1{-}0,2{-}1,3{-}2,4{-}3\}$	$\{1,0,3,4\}$
s_2	$\{4,5,6,7\}$	$\{5,0\}$	$\{5{-}0,0{-}1,0{-}2,0{-}3\}$	$\{5,6,7,0\}$
$\bar{s}_1$	$\{0,1,4,5\}$	$\{1,2,5,0\}$	$\{1{-}0,2{-}1,5{-}0,0{-}1\}$	$\{1,0,5,6\}$
s_1	$\{2,3,6,7\}$	$\{3,4,0\}$	$\{3{-}2,4{-}3,0{-}2,0{-}3\}$	$\{3,4,7,0\}$
$\bar{s}_0$	$\{0,2,4,6\}$	$\{1,3,5,0\}$	$\{1{-}0,3{-}2,5{-}0,0{-}2\}$	$\{1,3,5,7\}$
s_0	$\{1,3,5,7\}$	$\{2,4,0\}$	$\{2{-}1,4{-}3,0{-}1,0{-}3\}$	$\{4,6,0\}$

33

C. Dominik, *Embedding Sequential Circuits for their Polynomial Formal Verification*, BestMasters, https://doi.org/10.1007/978-3-658-50155-6_5

in the second column. The third column shows the sets obtained after applying the image computation to each initial set and the transition relation T, which describes the 3-bit mod-6 counter.

To compute the successor of state "$4 = 0b100$" based on this application of RDMC, the initial sets $S|_{s_2}$, $S|_{\overline{s}_1}$ and $S|_{\overline{s}_0}$ have to be examined. Similar to Example 4.1 and Example 4.2, the sets are illustrated in a FSM in Fig. 5.1(a). Set $S|_{s_2}$ is marked by diagonal lines, set $S|_{\overline{s}_1}$ by dots and set $S|_{\overline{s}_0}$ by horizontal lines. They overlap only in the state "100" which is marked in bold, similar to Example 4.2.

Using the corresponding resulting sets of the third column of Table 5.1, the successor is calculated with $\{5, 0\} \cap \{1, 2, 5, 0\} \cap \{1, 3, 5, 0\} = \{5, 0\}$. This intersection is depicted in Fig. 5.1(b). Now, the sets overlap in two states "000" and "101", as marked in bold.

This shows that RDMC cannot be applied in this case, because the intersection gives more than one state and therefore cannot be used to clearly distinguish the successor of state "4".

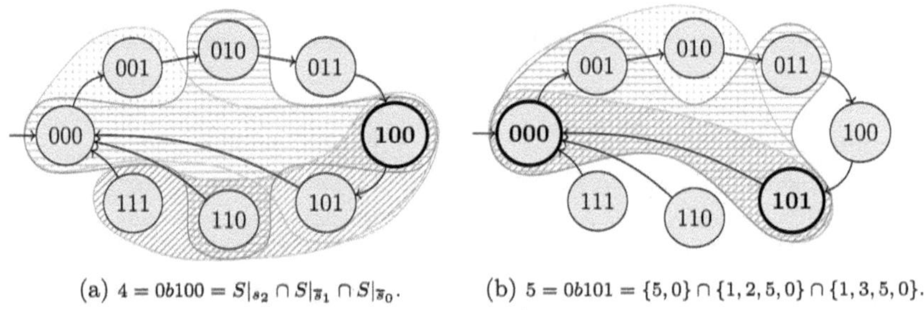

(a) $4 = 0b100 = S|_{s_2} \cap S|_{\overline{s}_1} \cap S|_{\overline{s}_0}$.   (b) $5 = 0b101 = \{5, 0\} \cap \{1, 2, 5, 0\} \cap \{1, 3, 5, 0\}$.

Fig. 5.1 FSMs of a 3-bit mod-6 counter with intersecting sets of states that give state "4" and its successor

5.1   Utilize Embedding

Since RDMC has distinctive results for bijective functions, it is a plausible approach to first turn a non-bijective function into a bijective one, before RDMC is applied. In Sect. 3.5, this transformation of a function has been introduced as embedding. But for an embedding, next to bijectivity the same number of inputs and outputs is required as well. Therefore an altered definition is needed.

Definition 5.1 *A function $he(f) : B^n \rightarrow B^{m+k}$ is the **half embedding** of a non-bijective function $f : B^n \rightarrow B^m$, if $he(f)$ results out of adding k garbage outputs to f so that it maps all n inputs to unique outputs. Compared to an embedding, this creates bijectivity instead of reversibility.*

Based on this definition, a non-bijective function can now be half embedded before it is verified, so that the results of RDMC are distinctive and contain meaningful information about the behavior of the function.

Example 5.2 *The half embedding of the 3-bit mod-6 counter, analyzed in Example 5.1, is visualized in Table 5.2:*

- *Table 4.1(a) is the truth table for the counter in the beginning, the current state bits are on the left side and the successor state bits on the right side. The last three transitions each reset the counter. Therefore, these transitions have equal successor state bits and the function is not injective. As explained in Sect. 3.5, this gives the maximum number of repetitions $M = 3$. Hence, to half embed the counter, at least two additional garbage outputs are needed to distinguish the three equal successor states.*
- *The truth table for the counter after one possible half embedding can be seen in Table 4.1(b). There, it is visible that together the two garbage outputs have a different value for each similar output pattern of the 3-bit mod-6 counter.*

The results of applying RDMC to this half embedded function are shown in the fourth column of Table 5.1. For each value, the successor state bits and garbage outputs are

Table 5.2 Truth tables for 3-bit mod-6 counter

(a) M_6C_3.

s_2	s_1	s_0	s_2'	s_1'	s_0'
0	0	0	0	0	1
0	0	1	0	1	0
0	1	0	0	1	1
0	1	1	1	0	0
1	0	0	1	0	1
1	0	1	0	0	0
1	1	0	0	0	0
1	1	1	0	0	0

(b) $he(M_6C_3)$.

s_2	s_1	s_0	s_2'	s_1'	s_0'	g_1	g_0
0	0	0	0	0	1	0	0
0	0	1	0	1	0	0	1
0	1	0	0	1	1	1	0
0	1	1	1	0	0	1	1
1	0	0	1	0	1	0	0
1	0	1	0	0	0	0	1
1	1	0	0	0	0	1	0
1	1	1	0	0	0	1	1

written as decimal numbers, separated by a hyphen. Compared to the 3-bit mod-6 counter of Example 5.1, the successor state of state "4" can now distinctively be computed as "5 − 0". Because the different successor states with value "0" can now be distinguished with the garbage outputs, not one of them is in every resulting set, which state "5 − 0" is a part of.

Lemma 5.1 *If RDMC is applied to a function $he(f) : B^n \rightarrow B^{m+k}$ that half embeds $f : B^n \rightarrow B^m$, the results are distinctive for any function f.*

Proof. As already stated in Sect. 4.1, for RDMC to be applicable, the following equality has to hold:

$$\forall q \in B^n : \bigcap_{\{I \mid I \in \mathbb{I} \wedge q \in I\}} image(I, T) = \{image(q, T)\}.$$

This is the case, if both "$\supseteq$" and "$\subseteq$" hold:

- "$\supseteq$": The resulting set contains at least the correct successor state, because $\forall q \in B^n : \bigcap_{\{I \mid I \in \mathbb{I} \wedge q \in I\}} I = \{q\}$ holds. This is not influenced by adding the garbage outputs.
- "$\subseteq$": The resulting set contains no other successor states, but the intended one, because $he(f)$ is bijective. Another successor state $p \in B^{m+k}$ with $he(f(q)) \neq p$ would be in the set, if all initial sets $I \in \mathbb{I}$, that contain the current state q, contain at least one other current state, which maps to p. If this was the case for f, garbage outputs were added for $he(f)$, so that no two initial states can map to the same successor state p. That way, at least one initial set $I \in \mathbb{I}$ with $q \in I$ cannot contain another state, which maps to p, because only the current state q is in all initial sets.

$\square$

5.2   Half Embedding based on BDDs

In the considered scenario, the modulo counter is given as a BDD. Therefore, a method is needed, that performs half embedding based on a BDD. Since half embedding only removes a step, which is needed for embedding, the general knowledge about embedding can still be used. But, the BDD-based method for embedding mentioned in Sect. 3.5 always assumes n garbage outputs. Reducing this could increase the overall runtime, especially if the method for half embedding and RDMC have different requirements, e.g. each works best with another state encoding. Then it would be more complicated to guarantee that the overall runtime stays polynomial. To reduce the number of garbage outputs anyway, a method for half embedding, that itself is based on RDMC, is proposed.

Definition 5.2 *The **RDMC-based half embedding** of an irreversible function $f(s_0, \ldots, s_{n-1}) : B^n \rightarrow B^m$ begins the same way as the algorithm described in Sect. 4.1:*

1. *First, $image(I, T)$ is computed for all $2 \cdot n$ sets $I \in \mathbb{I}$.*
2. *Then, garbage outputs g_i are added based on the resulting sets. The output g_i with $f(g_i) := s_i$ is added, if for s_i*

$$image(S|_{s_i}, T) \cap image(S|_{\overline{s}_i}, T) \neq \emptyset$$

holds. This means, if the intersection of the results for the two initial sets obtained by restricting the same variable s_i is not empty. The added output g_i is sorted directly after the corresponding s_i in the variable order, to minimize the nodes added.

Example 5.3 *The RDMC-based half embedding of a 3-bit mod-6 counter has the effect already discussed in Example 5.2. The two garbage outputs are gained from the resulting sets in the third column of Table 5.1:*

- *Output g_0 is added, because $\{1, 3, 5, 0\} \cap \{2, 4, 0\} = \{0\}$,*
- *output g_1 is added, because $\{1, 2, 5, 0\} \cap \{3, 4, 0\} = \{0\}$*
- *and no output g_3 is added, because $\{1, 2, 3, 4\} \cap \{5, 0\} = \emptyset$.*

The truth tables are therefore as shown in Table 5.2. The BDD for the original transition relation can be seen in Fig. 5.2. The BDD for the resulting, half embedded transition relation is shown in Fig. 5.3. It is visible in this example that it is efficient to have each g_i after the corresponding s_i in the variable order, because they have the same value and therefore the number of nodes needed is easier to estimate.

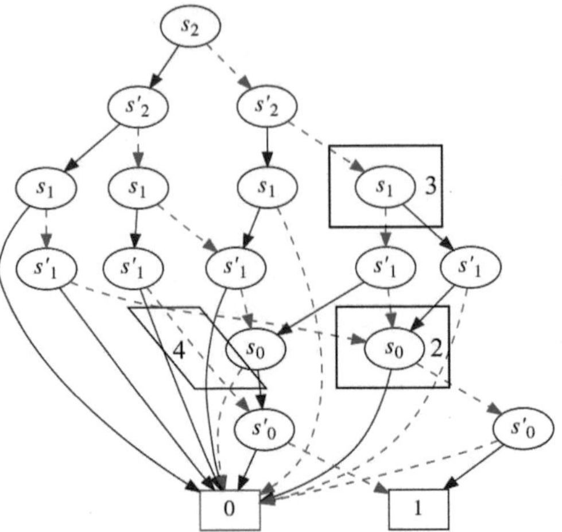

Fig. 5.2 Transition relation of a 3-bit mod-6 counter

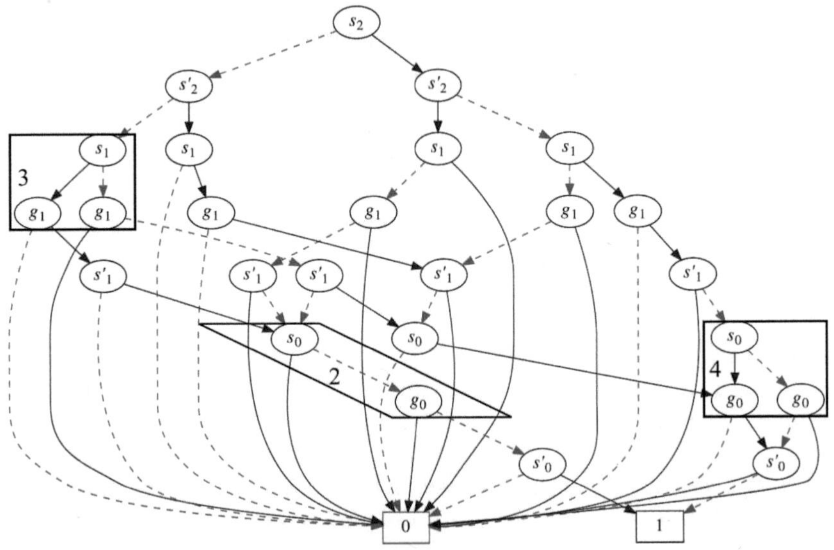

Fig. 5.3 Transition relation of a half embedded 3-bit mod-6 counter

Lemma 5.2 *Applying RDMC-based half embedding to an irreversible function* $f : B^n \rightarrow B^m$ *computes* $he(f)$.

Proof. To prove this, the resulting function always has to be bijective. Therefore, it has to be injective and surjective:

- It is easy to see that a function is **injective**, if the condition

$$image(S|_{s_i}, T) \cap image(S|_{\overline{s}_i}, T) \neq \emptyset$$

  for RDMC-half-embedding holds for all n current state variables s_i of the domain of f. Because then every s_i has the property that for some current states q with $s_i = 0$ and p with $s_i = 1$ and all remaining variables with arbitrary values, the sets these two values are mapped to must be disjunct. Therefore it is not possible to define two current states in such a way, that they map to the same value. Adding the garbage outputs ensures, that this property holds for all variables, for which is does not in the original f. This is the case, because s_i, which obviously has a different assignment in the two considered current states q and p, is passed on and can distinguish the two sets they are mapped to with that difference. Hence, the condition for RDMC-half-embedding then holds for all variables s_i in the domain of f and the resulting function must be injective.
- The resulting function is **surjective**, because the co-domain is exactly defined as the values, which the half embedded function maps to.

$\square$

To evaluate RDMC-based half embedding, it is compared to the BDD-based methods mentioned in Sect. 3.5 in the following. The method of [21] used to calculate M gives exact results, but not an entire embedding. It has been applied to a 3-bit mod-6 counter in Example 3.9. Comparing this to the application of RDMC-half-embedding to the same counter in Example 5.3, both methods suggest adding two garbage outputs. Further, comparing the BDDs of both examples in Fig. 3.5 and Fig. 5.2 shows that allowing any variable order for an embedding method can influence the BDD size, even if it is only slightly in this case. On the other hand, the second method of [21], that was mentioned, gives an entire embedding, but it adds $n = 3$ garbage outputs. Hence, the resulting BDD would be bigger. But in general, both embedding methods do not calculate an optimal embedding. RDMC-based half embedding may add more outputs than necessary as well, because the number of garbage outputs depends on the number of current state variables s_i, for which two input patterns q and p with the same assignment of s_i and equal $f(q)$ and $f(p)$ can be found. This means, the number of differences in input patterns, which are mapped to similar output patterns, is relevant. But M is defined based on the number of equal output patterns.

Example 5.4 *This can be demonstrated based on a modified 3-bit full counter. The corresponding truth table can be seen in Table 5.3(a). There, state "2" is mapped to state "0" and not to state "3". In the fifth column of Table 5.1, the resulting sets of each execution of RDMC are shown. As marked in bold, both sets for s_2 and both sets for s_1 contain the state "0". Hence, the garbage outputs g_2 and g_1 are added.*

The resulting truth table can be seen in Table 5.3(b). It is clear that only g_2 or only g_1 would have been sufficient to distinguish the equal output patterns, as both have the same value for the successor states "0". But the two current states "1" and "7", which are mapped to this output pattern, differ in two variables and this determines the garbage outputs.

Table 5.3 Truth tables for modified 3-bit full counter

(a) Modified FC_3.

s_2	s_1	s_0	s_2'	s_1'	s_0'
0	0	0	0	0	1
0	**0**	**1**	**0**	**0**	**0**
0	1	0	0	1	1
0	1	1	1	0	0
1	0	0	1	0	1
1	0	1	1	1	0
1	1	0	1	1	1
1	**1**	**1**	**0**	**0**	**0**

(b) Modified $he(FC_3)$.

s_2	s_1	s_0	s_2'	s_1'	s_0'	g_2	g_1
0	0	0	0	0	1	0	0
0	0	1	0	0	0	**0**	**0**
0	1	0	0	1	1	0	1
0	1	1	1	0	0	0	1
1	0	0	1	0	1	1	0
1	0	1	1	1	0	1	0
1	1	0	1	1	1	1	1
1	1	1	0	0	0	**1**	**1**

But as it was mentioned in Sect. 3.5, finding an optimal embedding is coNP-hard and can therefore not be achieved when aiming for PFV. With this goal in mind, RDMC-based half embedding is a suitable choice, because it can reduce the number of added garbage outputs compared to the embedding method of [21], without the resources that would be necessary for an optimal embedding. Example 3.2 already showed that the variable order can have a great effect on the size of a BDD. Hence, independence of a specific variable order is useful for PFV, as it can then be chosen in such a way that all BDDs are as small as possible. This is the case for both embedding methods.

But another valuable aspect of RDMC-based half embedding is that the entire verification process, consisting of the half embedding and the model checking, is based on RDMC. Therefore, any adjustment made to accelerate RDMC, e.g. to the representation of the transition relation, then benefits the runtime of the half embedding as well. The adjustments do not have to be balanced between the requirements of different underlying approaches. Further, if RDMC can be applied to some circuit within polynomial resources, it is very likely that the same holds for RDMC-half-embedding and vice versa.

5.3   RDMC-based Half Embedding of Modulo Counters

After introducing a more suitable method for half embedding in the previous Sect. 5.2, now the application of this method to modulo counters has to be analyzed. For this, the size of the BDD for the transition relation and an analysis of the used operations is necessary. This is then used to show that PFV of modulo counters is possible based on RDMC-based half embedding. The following Lemma has been proven as Lemma III.2 in [11]. The proof is given here as well, for a self-contained thesis and because it is needed for further explanations.

Lemma 5.3 *Let BDD T describe the transition relation of an n-bit modulo-m counter with the variables ordered as reversed pairs $(s_{n-1}, s'_{n-1}, s_n, s'_n, \ldots, s_0, s'_0)$. Then $|T| \leq 10 \cdot n$ holds.*

Proof. The BDD T is analyzed as in the proof of Lemma 4.1, where full counters were considered. Here, each current state q is viewed from MSB s_{n-1} to LSB s_0. Again, this divides the effect counting has on q into phases, of how each pair of variables (s_i, s'_i) depends on each other and on the previous phase. Further, an additional differentiation is necessary, because the counter resets several states q with $m - 1 \leq q < 2^n$ to "0", instead of only resetting state "$2^n - 1$".

1. **Counting up**: This applies to a state q with $0 \leq q < m - 1$. Traversing the variables of q consists of the following phases:

    (a) **The value is kept**: During this phase, the variables of state q are not yet affected by the counting, hence a successor state variable s'_i is set to the value of the corresponding current state variable s_i. Like for the full counter, this is described by the component $s_i s'_i + \overline{s}_i \overline{s}'_i$. But since the order of pairs is reversed, this happens in the first phase and the transition from Phase 1(a) to Phase 1(b) is given by the component $\overline{s}_i s'_i$.

(b) **The value is flipped**: Once the values of a state q are affected by the counting, each s_i' takes the opposite value of s_i. This phase is initiated by flipping a value from "0" to "1" described by the component $\overline{s}_i s_i'$. If this phase is not initiated for the top variable s_{n-1}, this component is the transition from Phase 1(a) to Phase 1(b). After that, the phase is described by the component $s_i \overline{s}_i'$. Hence, this phase is reversed compared to a full counter.

(c) **The value is kept for states similar to** $m-1$: A state q can have a beginning, which is similar to the beginning of the maximum value of the counter $m-1$, when read from MSB to LSB. Such states have to be considered separately, by only keeping the values of this similar beginning with either the component $s_i s_i'$ or the component $\overline{s}_i \overline{s}_i'$. The nodes of Phase 1(a) cannot be used for this, because only one of both possible values is kept. For the other value, the state would be reset. If this distinction between counting and resetting is clear for all states for the given m at some point of the traversal, this phase is merged with Phase 1(a).

Since Phase 1(a) and Phase 1(b) are similar to the phases described in the proof of Lemma 4.1, this needs fives nodes for each variables pair (s_i, s_i') as well. Two additional nodes are used for Phase 2.

2. **Resetting**: This applies to a state q with $m - 1 \leq q < 2^n$. The phases when traversing the variables of state q are:

(a) **The value is reset for states similar to** $m - 1$: Analogously to Phase 1(c), the reset of the state $m - 1$ and a state q with a similar beginning is described separately with either $s_i \overline{s}_i'$ or $\overline{s}_i \overline{s}_i'$. Once q has a different value of s_i than $m - 1$ at some point of the traversal, it transitions to Phase 2(b) without additional nodes. This phase is merged as a whole with Phase 2(b), if this is clear for all states at this point.

(b) **The value is reset**: All remaining variables of a state q in this phase are reset to 0. This is described by the component $(s_i + \overline{s}_i)\overline{s}_i'$.

Phase 2(a) needs two nodes and Phase 2(b) only one. Hence, for each pair of variables (s_i, s_i') the reset takes three nodes.

Overall this results in at most ten nodes for each pair of variables (s_i, s_i'), therefore at most $10 \cdot n$ nodes are used in T.

$\square$

Example 5.5 *The different components of the transition relation of an n-bit modulo-m counter with variables ordered as reversed pairs, as described in the proof of Lemma 5.3, cannot be seen clearly enough for the values $n < 5$. Hence, the transition of an n-bit modulo-m counter with $n = 5$ and $m = 18$ is chosen for this example and can be seen in Fig. 5.4. Each component is marked for the pair (s_2, s_2'):*

- *Phase 1(a) and Phase 1(b) are very similar to the ones of full counters discussed in Example 4.4.*
- *The additional separation of Phase 1(c) is very clear in this example. Because the considered counter has the maximum value $17 = 0b10001$, the only state below it with a similar beginning is state $16 = 0b10000$. Hence, Phase 1(c) holds for almost this entire state. Only for the last pair (s_0, s_0'), it is merged into Phase 1(a).*
- *Analogously, Phase 2(a) and Phase 2(b) are separated very clearly for this example, because Phase 2(a) only applies to the maximum value $17 = 0b10001$ itself.*

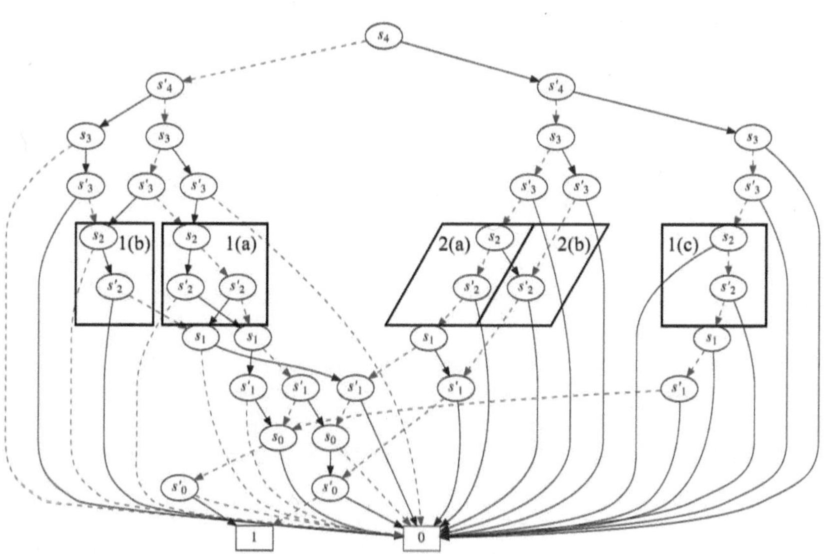

Fig. 5.4 Transition relation of a 5-bit mod-18 counter with variables ordered as reversed pairs

Overall, the BDD has 36 nodes, which is less than the maximum number of nodes
$10 \cdot 5 = 50$ *named in Lemma 5.3. The difference between the BDD size and its*
maximum size is bigger compared to Example 4.4, because for modulo counters
phases can be merged, which creates additional redundancies.

Example 5.6 *Compared to Example 5.5, the transition relation of an n-bit modulo-*
m counter with $n = 5$ *and* $m = 18$ *and no variable reordering can be seen in Fig. 5.5.*
With overall 68 nodes, 32 additional nodes are needed with respect to the 36 nodes
of same counter when variables are ordered as reversed pairs as in Example 5.5.
This further demonstrates the importance of choosing a suitable variable order.

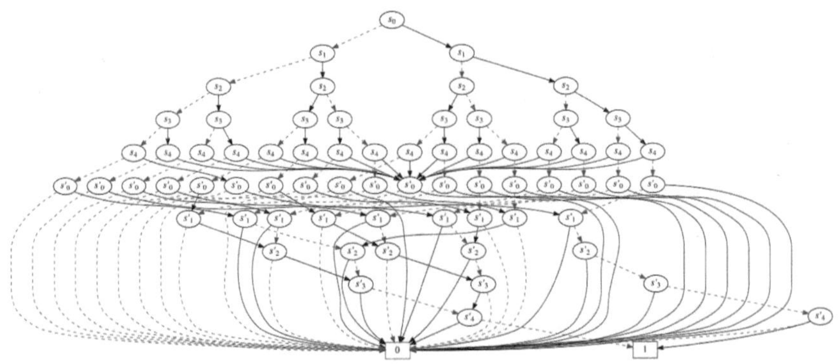

Fig. 5.5 Transition relation of a 5-bit mod-18 counter with no variable reordering

Compared to the verification of full counters in Chap. 4, a different variable
order is used. If a pair-wise variable order would be used as well, the separation
of counting and resetting would be less clear. An additional node in T would be
necessary for each pair (s_i, s_i'), to distinguish if flipping a variable from "1" to "0"
belongs to counting or resetting. This would increase the upper bound of Lemma 5.3
to $11 \cdot n$. Even if this is only a slight difference, this underlines that it is an advantage,
if the embedding method can be applied to a BDD of any variable order.

Example 5.7 *Compared to Example 5.5, the transition relation of an n-bit modulo-*
m counter with $n = 5$ *and* $m = 18$ *and variables ordered as pairs can be seen in*
Fig. 5.6. The equivalent nodes for the phases of the proof of Lemma 5.3 are marked
for pair (s_2, s_2'). *The additional node is marked with a dotted outline.*

A path in the BDD is visible, that starts in Phase 1(b), passes this additional node and ends in Phase 2. This shows, that the extra node is caused by separating the flipping of a variable of Phase 2 from the flipping of Phase 1. Hence, the separation of both phases is less clear in the BDD.

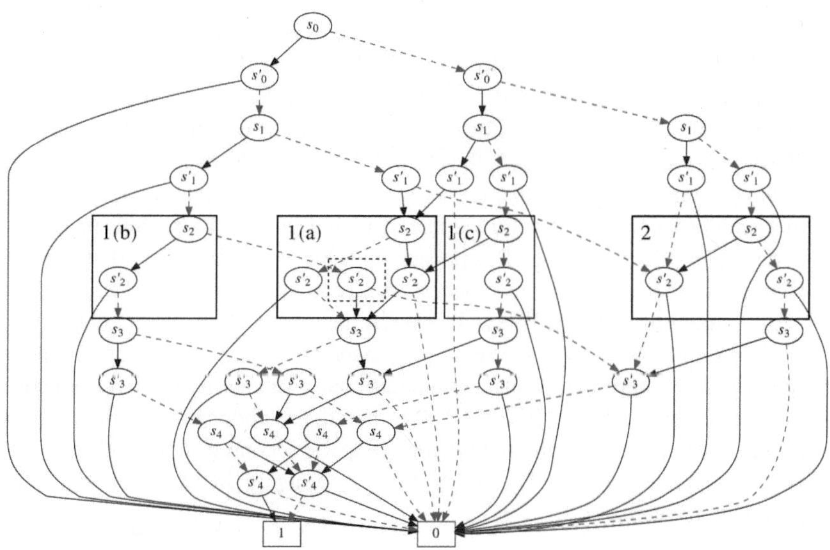

Fig. 5.6 Transition relation of a 5-bit mod-18 counter with pair-wise ordering

Definition 5.3 *Let an **on-set redundancy** in a BDD be a reduced, redundant node v, for which the high child, and hence the low child too, are not the "0"-terminal. Otherwise it is an **off-set redundancy**.*

Lemma 5.4 *Let BDD T describe the transition relation of an n-bit modulo-m counter and $he(T)$ the RDMC-half-embedding of T, both with variables ordered as reversed pairs. Then $|he(T)| \leq 2 \cdot (|T| + n)$ holds.*

Proof. During the RDMC-half-embedding of T, the effect of adding a garbage output g_i with $g_i := s_i$ after the corresponding state variable s_i is one of the four following cases for every specific s_i-node:

1. **No nodes are added:** This is the case, if the s_i-node is an off-set redundancy. This means, this node was reduced, because its high and low child are both the "0"-terminal. Any g_i-node added would therefore lead to the "0"-terminal with both children as well, and hence would be another off-set redundancy.

2. **One node is added:** This is the case, if the s_i-node leads to an internal node or the "1"-terminal with one edge and to the "0"-terminal with the other. The g_i-node copying the value of the s_i-node, which leads to the "0"-terminal, is an off-set redundancy because of the same reasoning as in Case 1. The g_i-node copying the other value basically replaces the s_i-node. The s_i-node then instead points to the g_i-node with the same edge, with which it previously pointed to the internal node or, respectively, the "1"-terminal. Hence, this adds one node.

3. **Two nodes are added:** This is the case, if the s_i-node leads to an internal node or the "1"-terminal with both edges. Then, both values of the s_i-node are copied in a similar way as the second value considered in Case 2. But since each g_i-node copies only one value, the opposite edge always leads to the "0"-terminal. Hence two additional nodes are necessary to copy both values of the s_i-node.

4. **Three nodes are added:** This is the case, if the s_i-node is an on-set redundancy. The high and low child of the reduced s_i-node are both the same internal node or both the "1"-terminal. Hence, two additional g_i-nodes are necessary to copy both values, as described in Case 3. But then the s_i-node points with one edge to the first g_i-node and with the other edge to the second g_i-node and therefore is not redundant anymore. By adding this s_i-node again, in total three additional nodes are needed.

Now, T has to be analyzed further, to determine which of the cases hold and how often. A detailed description of T is given in the proof of Lemma 5.3. Here, the following two properties are relevant:

1. **The only on-set redundancies in T are at most n current state nodes s_i.** A variable v is an on-set redundancy, only if some assignment for all other variables satisfies the function independent of the value of v. Therefore, there are none in the transition relation of a full counter, because each current state maps to a different successor state. This means, any two satisfying assignments must have different values for at least two variables, this is for at least one current state variable and at least one successor state variable. But for T several states map to the state, where all variables are reset to "0". It was described in the proof of Lemma 5.3 that Phase 2(b) represents all these resets. This results in one path in T, where starting with some current state variable s_i all remaining ones until s_0 are reset to 0. This path is given by $(s_i + \bar{s}_i)\bar{s}'_i \ldots (s_0 + \bar{s}_0)\bar{s}'_0$, where all current

state variables are on-set redundancies. The top-most node this path can start with is s_{n-1}, therefore it can at most contain n pairs (s_i, s_i') and hence at most n on-set redundancies.

2. **The number of current state nodes in T, after the on-set redundancies are removed, is never greater than the number of successor state nodes.** The structure of T with a worst-case size is described in detail in the proof of Lemma 5.3. While T does not need all the nodes mentioned there for every possible modulo value, it still always consists out of the same components for each pair (s_i, s_i'). The components, describing the different aspects of modulo counting for each pair, consist of either less or just as many s_i-nodes compared to s_i'-nodes. If this holds for any pair of s_i and s_i' in T, it must overall hold for T as well.

Out of Property 1 follows that Case 3 is applied at most n times. Therefore, at most n current state nodes are added to T and, after that, for each current state node at most two garbage nodes are added. This would mean, $2 \cdot (|T| + n)$ additional garbage nodes are needed. But Property 2 indicates that at most half of T are current state nodes, after the on-set redundancies are removed. Combined, those two properties consequently imply that at most $|T| + n$ garbage outputs are necessary. Overall this results in at most $2 \cdot (|T| + n)$ nodes in $he(T)$.

$\square$

Example 5.8 *The transition relation of an RDMC-half-embedded n-bit modulo-m counter with $n = 3$ and $m = 6$ can be seen in Fig. 5.3. It consists of 26 nodes. Compared to this, the transition relation of this counter before the half embedding in Fig. 5.2 consists of 16 nodes. Hence, the size of the half embedded counter is less than the maximum of $2 \cdot 16 = 32$ named in Lemma 5.4. The different cases mentioned in the proof of Lemma 5.4 can be seen when comparing Fig. 5.2 and Fig. 5.3. In both, examples for Case 2, Case 3 and Case 4 are marked. Examples for Case 1 can easily be found. Further, the different properties become visible in Fig. 5.2. The only on-set redundancy is an s_0-node and overall 7 s_i-nodes are used, 1 s_i-node is an on-set redundancy and 9 s_i'-nodes are used.*

Example 5.9 *The transition relation of an RDMC-half-embedded n-bit modulo-m counter with $n = 3$ and $m = 6$ and garbage nodes added at the end can be seen in Fig. 5.7. Compared to Example 5.8, 3 additional nodes are needed, which supports the choice of sorting the garbage outputs close to the variable they copy.*

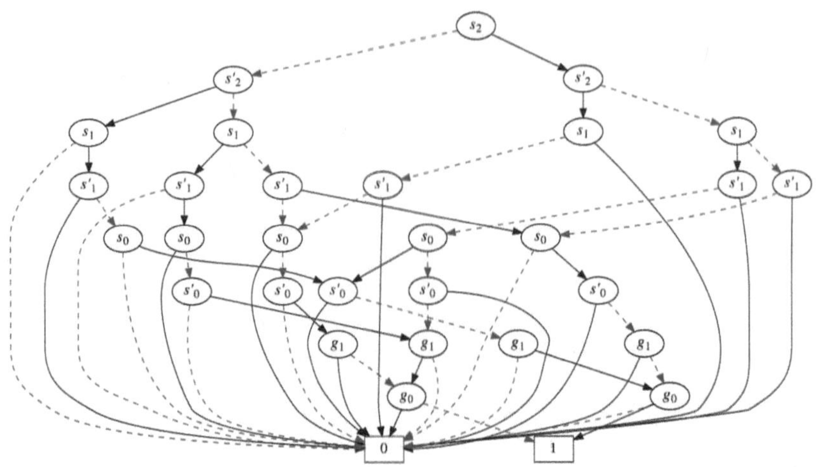

Fig. 5.7 Transition relation of a half embedded 3-bit mod-6 counter with garbage outputs at the end

After analyzing the BDDs for the transition relations appearing in the RDMC-based half embedding, now the needed resources can be determined. As already mentioned in Sect. 4.2, the relevant operations to examine for RDMC are "$\wedge$" and "$\exists$". For evaluating the steps needed for "$\wedge$", the previous contributions about the size of the occuring BDDs are sufficient. But a closer look at the operation "$\exists$" has to be taken as well. Hence, this is an essential part of the proof of the following theorem.

Theorem 5.1 *The time and space demands of RDMC-based half embedding of an n-bit modulo-m counter with variables ordered as reversed pairs are in $\mathcal{O}(n^2)$ and $\mathcal{O}(n)$, respectively.*

Proof. The approach to the analysis of the required resources begins similar to the one used in the proof of Theorem 4.1. Each step of RDMC-based half embedding, as specified in Definition 5.2, is considered in detail:

1. **Operation** *image*(I, T)**:** This operation is applied first. The steps are, as given in Sect. 3.2:

(a) **Conjunction $I \wedge T$:** The argumentation is analogous to the proof of Theorem 4.1, therefore the runtime and size of the result are in $\mathcal{O}(|T|)$.

(b) **Quantification $\exists S$:** In general, the argumentation is analogous as well. But it has to be shown that the result of each quantification has a size smaller or equal to $|T|$, because T now consists of different components.

The nodes in S are quantified going from s_0 to s_{n-1}, this means in a bottom-up order. Hence, executing $\exists s_i \, G$ does not affect any of the above nodes $s_{n-1}, s'_{n-1}, \ldots, s_{i+1}, s'_{i+1}$. The execution removes all s_i-nodes and all current state variables below $s_{i-1}, \ldots, s_0$ have been removed in the previous quantifications. Only the remaining successor state variables below s'_j with $0 \leq j < i$ have to be analyzed further. Compared to T, the number of nodes per s'_j is always equal or decreased by applying $\exists s_i \, G$. This effect can be seen based on the structure of the considered circuit described in the proof of Lemma 5.3. Similar to the proof of Theorem 4.1, components $s_i s'_i + \bar{s}_i \bar{s}'_i$ and $(s_i + \bar{s}_i) \bar{s}'_i$ can be split up, if only one part of the component is selected by Step 1(a).

   i. **Components for exclusively keeping or resetting a single value:** Those are e.g. $s_i s'_i$ or $s_i \bar{s}'_i$. With respect to the proof of Lemma 5.3, this includes the components of Phase 1(b), Phase 1(c) and Phase 2(a) and the component with which Phase 1(b) is entered. It further includes the already mentioned parts of components. When $G|_{\bar{s}_i} \vee G|_{s_i}$ is applied to such a component, one of the operands leads to the "0"-terminal. This operand is the value of the successor state, which is not kept or not the reset value. Hence, only the subgraph of the other operand is kept.

   ii. **Component for resetting any value:** This is done with $(s_i + \bar{s}_i) \bar{s}'_i$ during Phase 2(b). The component is unaffected, because the s_i-node is already removed.

   iii. **Component for keeping any value:** During Phase 1(a) this is done with $s_i s'_i + \bar{s}_i \bar{s}'_i$, which results in $s'_i + \bar{s}'_i$. This therefore creates a path of redundant successor state nodes.

Throughout the repeated application of "$\exists$", this does not result in a continuous decrease in size, but compared to T, no new nodes for s'_j can be created. Only by splitting the component $(s_i + \bar{s}_i) \bar{s}'_i$ during Step 1(a), a node can be added to T by removing the redundancy. But as discussed in Lemma 5.4, at most n of these redundancies exist. This proves, applying $\exists S \, G$ creates no intermediate or final BDD bigger than T and each application has a number of steps in $\mathcal{O}(|T|^2)$.

(c) **Substitution *rename*:** The argumentation is analogous to the proof of Theorem 4.1. Hence, this step is in $\mathcal{O}(|T|)$.

Similar to the proof of Theorem 4.1, Step 1 is applied $2 \cdot n$ times and each operation has a runtime in $\mathcal{O}(|T|^2)$. Step 1 therefore must be executable with a number of steps in $\mathcal{O}(|T|^2)$.

2. **Add garbage outputs:** As given in Definition 5.2, three steps are necessary for this:

   (a) **Intersection:** To compute the intersection of two sets computed by Step 1 $image(S|_{s_i}, T)$ and $image(S|_{\bar{s}_i}, T)$, they are combined with "$\wedge$". As proven in Step 1(b), the size of both sets is in $\mathcal{O}(|T|)$. The intersection hence needs a number of steps in $\mathcal{O}(|T|^2)$. Since a modulo counter is considered, the result is either the set $\emptyset$ or the set $\{0\}$. Both have a size in $\mathcal{O}(1)$.
   (b) **Comparison with $\emptyset$:** As explained in Sect. 3.1, BDDs are canonical, therefore it is only necessary for this step to simply check, if the result of Step 2(a) is equal to the "0"-terminal.
   (c) **Add g_i if indicated by Step 2(b):** Any g_i is added with the operation $T \wedge g_i$. Again, the runtime for this and the size of the result is in $\mathcal{O}(|T|)$, because the BDD for g_i is only one node. At most n garbage outputs can be added, hence this statement still holds, even if all possible garbage outputs are necessary.

   These steps are applied for any s_i to the initial sets $image(S|_{s_i}, T)$ and $image(S|_{\bar{s}_i}, T)$. Hence, the three operations 2(a) to 2(c) are executed n times. Considering the runtime necessary for each of them, the required number of steps overall is in $\mathcal{O}(|T|^2)$.

The maximum runtime during this analysis is $\mathcal{O}(|T|^2)$. $|T|$ is less than or equal to $10 \cdot n$ according to Lemma 5.3. This shows that the overall time demands must be in $\mathcal{O}(n^2)$.

To minimize the number of BDDs stored simultaneously, the half embedding can be carried out fully for each pair of $S|_{s_i}$ and $S|_{\bar{s}_i}$ in $\mathbb{I}$, instead of first applying Step 1 to all $I \in \mathbb{I}$ and then applying Step 2 to the results. Then the only BDDs needed for the entire computation are T and $he(T)$. T has a size less than or equal to $10 \cdot n$ and according to Lemma 5.4 $|he(T)| \leq 2 \cdot (|T| + n)$ holds. Hence, $he(T)$ has a size less than or equal to $22 \cdot n$. During Step 1 at most three additional BDDs with a size in $\mathcal{O}(|T|)$ are used in parallel. For Step 2 at most the two results of Step 1 are needed simultaneously. This concludes that the overall space demands are in $\mathcal{O}(n)$. $\qquad\qquad\square$

5.4 **PFV of Half Embedded Modulo Counters**

In the previous section it was proven that any modulo counter can be half embedded within polynomial resources. Based on this, now the resources needed for the verification of these half embedded modulo counters can be analyzed.

Theorem 5.2 *The time and space demands of RDMC of a RDMC-half-embedded n-bit modulo-m counter with variables ordered as reversed pairs are in $\mathcal{O}(n^2)$ and $\mathcal{O}(n)$, respectively.*

Proof. The proof is very similar to the proof of Theorem 4.1. Step 1 to Step 3 can equally be applied here as well, replacing T with $he(T)$. The intermediate results of Step 2 also do not exceed $he(T)$ in size, despite of the additional garbage outputs. If $\exists s_i$ is applied, a garbage output copying both values with $s_i g_i + \overline{s}_i \overline{g}_i$ becomes redundant and is removed. A garbage output copying only one value with $s_i g_i$ or $\overline{s}_i \overline{g}_i$ takes the place of the s_i-node. Hence, no further nodes can be added. Only $he(T)$ and the final results of each execution of Step 1 are kept throughout the entire computation, therefore at most $2 \cdot n$ BDDs with a size in $\mathcal{O}(|he(T)|)$ are stored in parallel. $|he(T)|$ has been shown in Lemma 5.4 to be less than or equal to $2 \cdot (|T|+n)$. According to Lemma 5.3, $|T|$ is less than or equal to $10 \cdot n$. Considering all these statements, the number of steps needed for applying RDMC is in $\mathcal{O}(n^2)$ and the upper bound for memory usage is given by $\mathcal{O}(n)$.

$\square$

With this, the goal of this section is accomplished. With the RDMC-based half embedding of an n-bit modulo-m counter, followed by its verification using RDMC, a complete verification procedure has been proposed. The polynomial bounds proven in Theorem 5.1 and Theorem 5.2 ensure the efficiency of this procedure. This proves PFV for any n-bit modulo-m counter.

Experimental Results **6**

The concepts discussed in the previous sections of this thesis have been implemented, to confirm the theoretical results. All computations have been realized in C++ and CUDD [23] was used for BDD operations. The setup has a 3.6 GHz AMD Ryzen 5 CPU and 16 GB RAM.

6.1 Full Counter Circuits

For the implementation of the verification of n-bit full counter circuits, as described in Sect. 4, the algorithm for SMC and RDMC were followed. As stated there, all variables were ordered as pairs.

6.1.1 Symbolic Model Checking

First, the algorithm for SMC, which is explained in Sect. 3.2, was applied to full counters for different values n with $1 \leq n \leq 30$. The size of each BDD computed during each execution was measured. The results are visualized in Fig. 6.1. The size of the transition relation T for each n is shown with circles. For comparison the function $5 \cdot n$ was added as a dashed line. Of all intermediate BDDs computed during one execution, the peak size is marked with crosses. The following aspects can be observed:

- The size of T is always slightly below the reference function $5 \cdot n$, which underlines the statement of Lemma 4.1.
- As anticipated, there is no blow-up in size during the computation, since the crosses are always below the other two graphs.

C. Dominik, *Embedding Sequential Circuits for their Polynomial Formal Verification*, BestMasters, https://doi.org/10.1007/978-3-658-50155-6_6

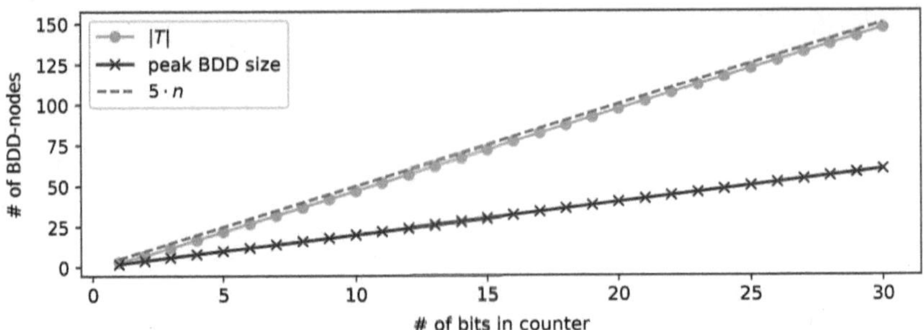

Fig. 6.1 BDD sizes during SMC of full n-bit counter for different n

Figure 6.2 shows the runtime of the execution for each n as a solid line. The duration is measured in hours. For $n = 30$ this is already close to 3 hours. For comparison, the function $a \cdot 2^n$ was added as a dashed line. The variable a with $a = 0.000000003$ is necessary, so that the measured times can be compared to this reference function, which grows exponentially with respect to n. Naturally, the time and number of variables do not have the same scale and need to be normalized to be comparable. Hence, a can be seen as the ration between n and hours. This exponential reference function is very similar to the growth of the measured times. Overall this underlines the statement that SMC has a runtime exponential in n for full counters. The measurements show that SMC is not feasible for circuits with an exponential sequential depth.

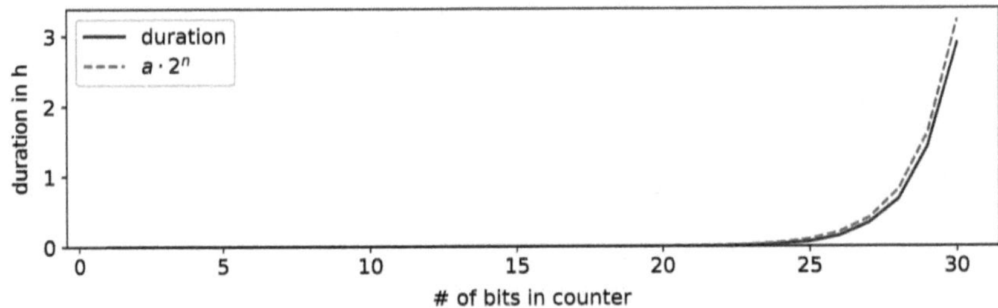

Fig. 6.2 Duration during SMC of full n-bit counter for different n

6.1.2 Restricted Domain Model Checking

In a second step, the algorithm for RDMC, as described in Sect. 4 was analyzed. Here, the verification was executed for different values n with $1 \leq n \leq 1024$. The measured BDD sizes can be seen in Fig. 6.3. Analogously, the size of T is marked with circles and a dashed line represents $5 \cdot n$. The peak size of intermediate BDDs is again given by crosses. Similarly, the following can be observed:

- The size of T and the reference function $5 \cdot n$ are very close, which extends the results given by Fig. 6.1 to a higher n.

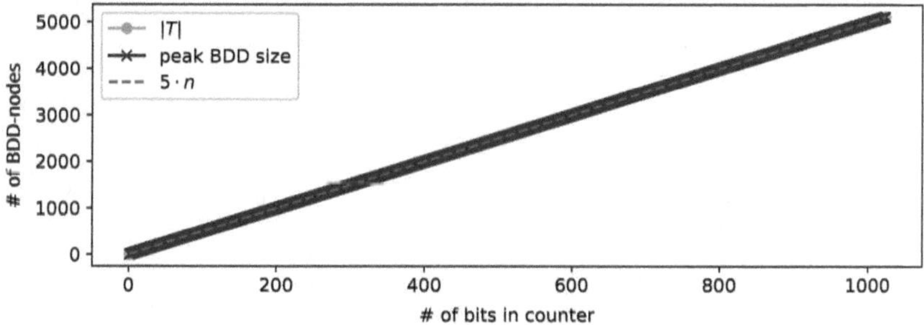

Fig. 6.3 BDD sizes during RDMC of full n-bit counter for different n

- This time, the peak size of intermediate BDDs is equal to $|T|$. As predicted in Theorem 4.1, this shows that the size of all BDDs created is in $\mathcal{O}(|T|)$ and therefore there is no blow-up in size exceeding $|T|$.

The measured duration for each execution is depicted in Fig. 6.4 as a solid line. The time is measured in seconds. It is obvious already at a first glance that the runtime is fundamentally improved by applying RDMC instead of SMC. It was possible to verify counters with a considerably higher n and even for $n = 1024$, the verification only took 31 seconds. Further, the growth of time is polynomial with respect to n. This can be seen by comparing the graph to the dashed line for the function $a \cdot n^2$. Again, a was added to align the number of variables to the scale in seconds. Here, $a = 0.00004$ was used. The similarity in growth of both graphs underlines the polynomial bounds for the runtime given by Theorem 4.1.

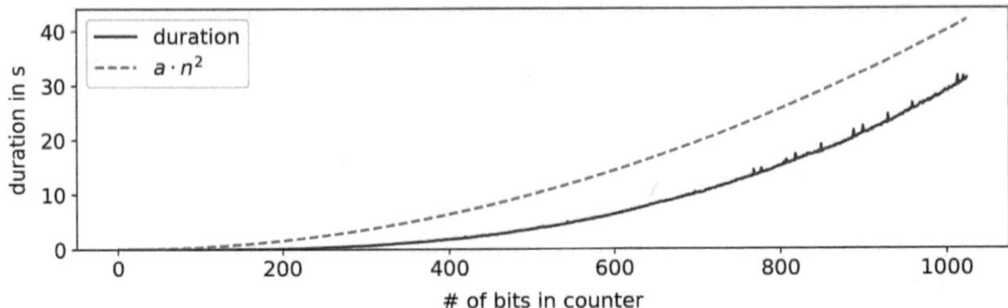

Fig. 6.4 Duration during RDMC of full n-bit counter for different n

6.2   Modulo Counter Circuits

The verification of n-bit modulo-m counter circuits has been implemented according to the concepts discussed in Chap. 5. This includes the RDMC-based half embedding as given in Sect. 5.2 and, afterwards, the algorithm for RDMC, as it has already been applied to full counters in the previous Sect. 6.1. The variables were ordered as reversed pairs.

6.2.1   Fixed Number of Variables

In a first step, the implementation was executed for a fixed number of variables n and all possible modulo values m with $1 < m \leq 2^n$. The measured BDD sizes can be seen in Fig. 6.5 for a 4-bit modulo counter, set in relation to the modulo values $1 < m \leq 16$. Analogously, BDD sizes during the computation for an 8-bit modulo counter and modulo values $1 < m \leq 256$ can be seen in Fig. 6.6. Since this covers an exponential number of values, this was not computed for values of $n > 14$. In both plots, the size of the transition relation T is marked with squares, the size of the RDMC-half-embedding of T is depicted with circles. A dashed line shows the maximum bound for the size of $he(T)$, which was given by Lemma 5.4 as $2 \cdot (|T| + n)$. Further, the peak BDD size of intermediate results, that occur during the verification, is shown as crosses. The peak BDD size of intermediate results during the half embedding is shown as triangles. The following aspects become visible:

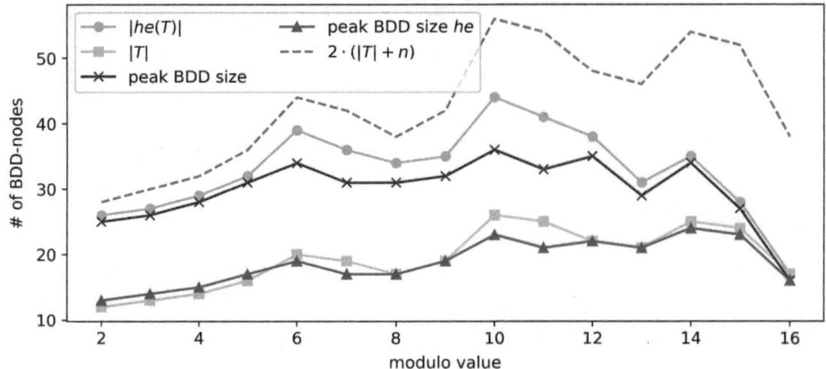

Fig. 6.5 BDD sizes for different m during RDMC of 4-bit modulo-m counter

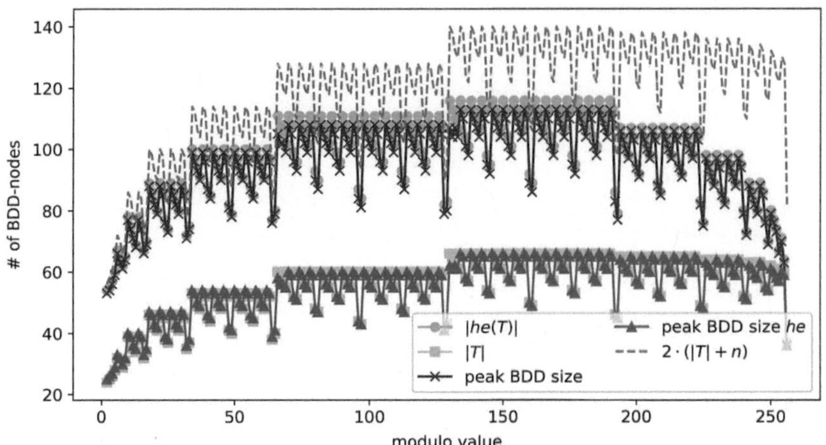

Fig. 6.6 BDD sizes for different m during RDMC of 8-bit modulo-m counter

- For smaller modulo values, like $1 < m \leq 8$ in Fig. 6.5 or $1 < m \leq 16$ in Fig. 6.6, the measured $|he(T)|$ are close to the upper bound $2 \cdot (|T| + n)$, but the gap increases, as m approaches its maximum value. Especially, no value for $|he(T)|$ is computed, that is higher than the upper bound, which underlines the statement of Lemma 5.4.

- The peak BDD size during verification is close to the size of $he(T)$, but never exceeds it, as was predicted in the proof of Theorem 5.2.

- For modulo values $1 < m \leq 2^{n-2} + 1$ the peak BDD size during embedding exceeds $|T|$ by one node, for the remaining values of m it is equal to $|T|$ or below it. This confirms the statement of Theorem 5.1 that the space demands for half embedding are in $\mathcal{O}(|T|)$.

As additional examples, the BDD sizes for $n = 3$ can be found in Fig. 6.7, for $n = 6$ in Fig. 6.8, for $n = 10$ in Fig. 6.9, for $n = 12$ in Fig. 6.10 and for $n = 14$ in Fig. 6.11. The results are very similar.

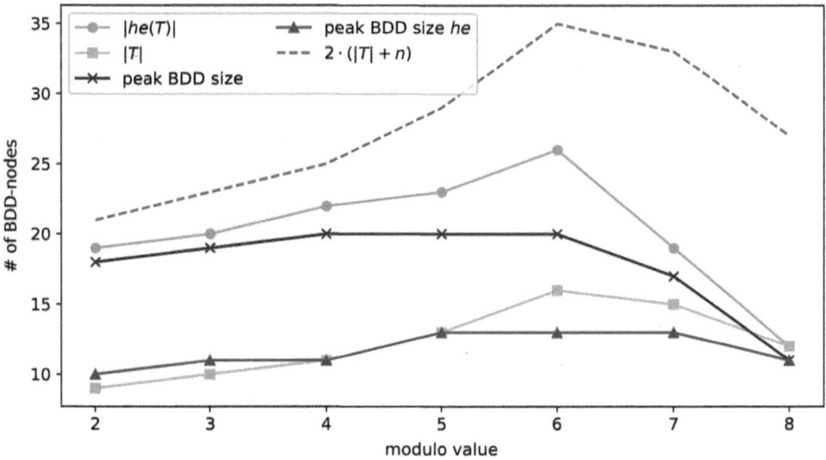

Fig. 6.7 BDD sizes for different m during RDMC of 3-bit modulo-m counter

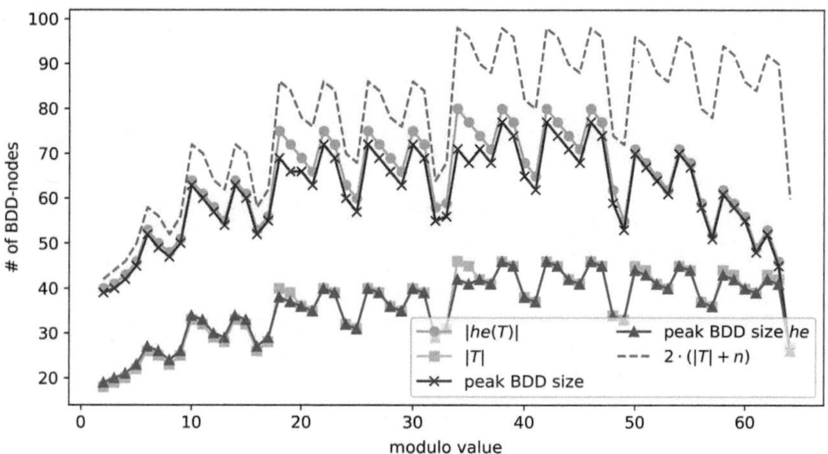

Fig. 6.8 BDD sizes for different m during RDMC of 6-bit modulo-m counter

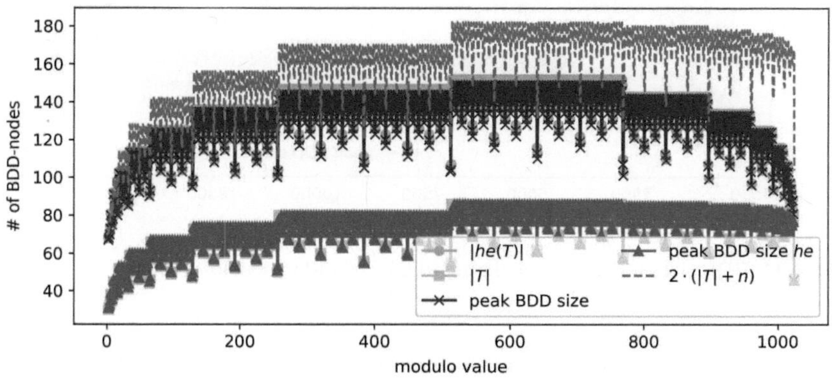

Fig. 6.9 BDD sizes for different m during RDMC of 10-bit modulo-m counter

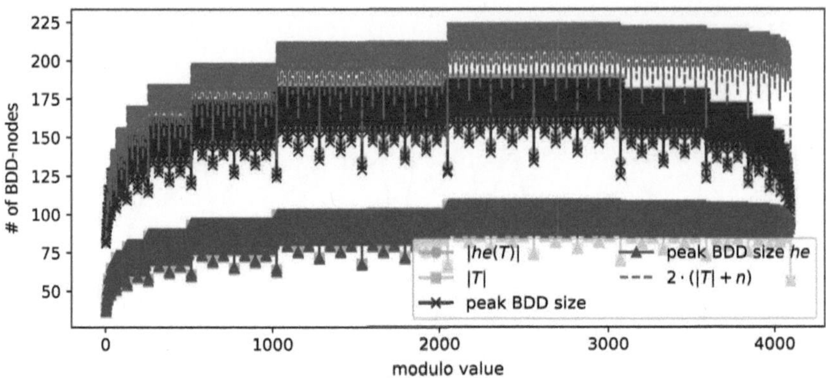

Fig. 6.10 BDD sizes for different m during RDMC of 12-bit modulo-m counter

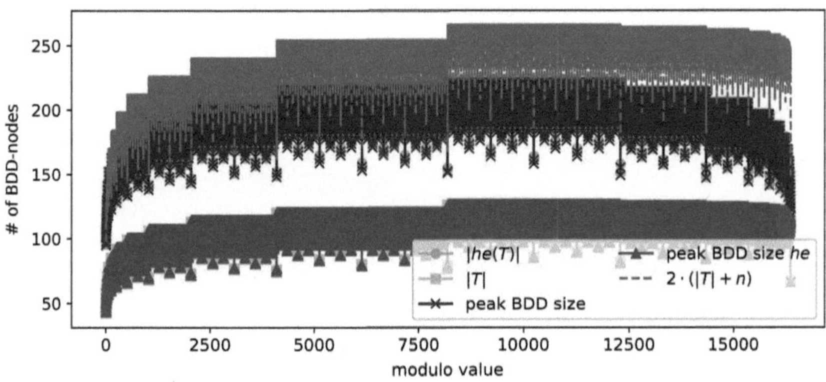

Fig. 6.11 BDD sizes for different m during RDMC of 14-bit modulo-m counter

The runtime needed for the verification has been measured as well. This can be seen in Fig. 6.12 for a 14-bit modulo-m counter with $1 < m \leq 16384$. The graph shows the time measured in milliseconds with respect to each modulo value. The duration of the RDMC-based half embedding is depicted by a dotted line, the duration of the verification with RDMC by a solid line. Except for some measuring inaccuracies, which are likely to occur when using such a high precision, the embedding is executed in less than 10 milliseconds for each modulo value m, and the verification in less than 3 milliseconds. The polynomial bounds given for the runtime in Theorem 5.1 and Theorem 5.2 cannot be seen here, because the value for n is fixed. But it shows the efficiency of the verification process.

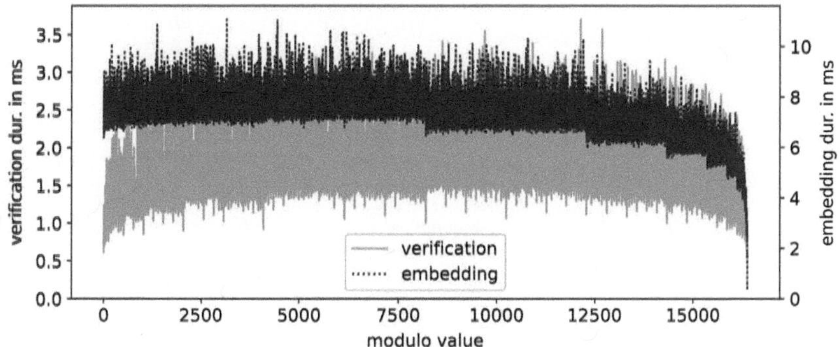

Fig. 6.12 Duration for different m during RDMC of 14-bit modulo-m counter

Analogous examples for $n = 4$ with runtimes below 3 milliseconds can be found in Fig. 6.13, for $n = 8$ with runtimes below 6 milliseconds Fig. 6.14, for $n = 10$ with runtimes below 8 milliseconds in Fig. 6.15 and for $n = 12$ with runtimes below 9 milliseconds in Fig. 6.16.

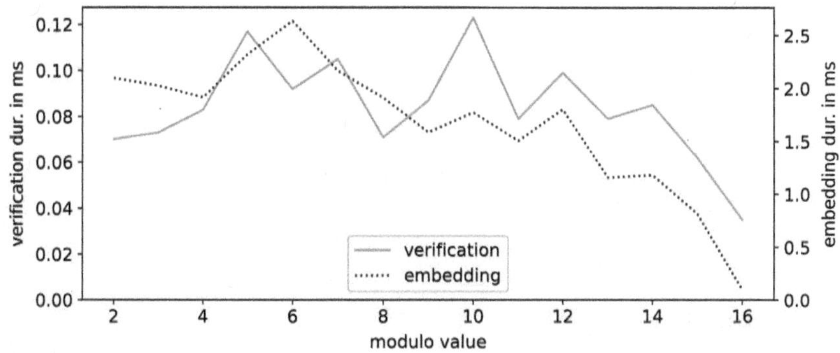

Fig. 6.13 Duration for different m during RDMC of 4-bit modulo-m counter

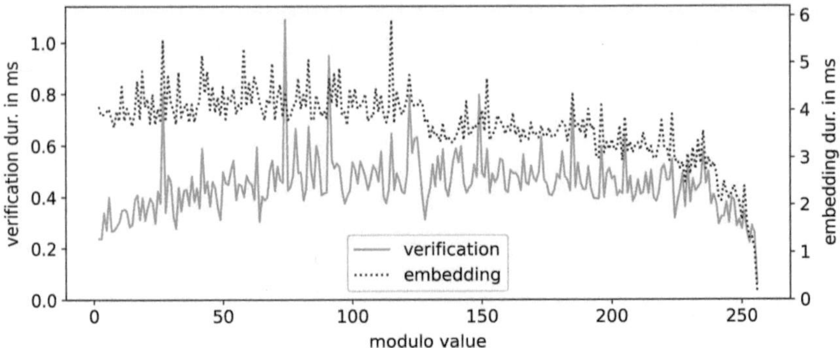

Fig. 6.14 Duration for different m during RDMC of 8-bit modulo-m counter

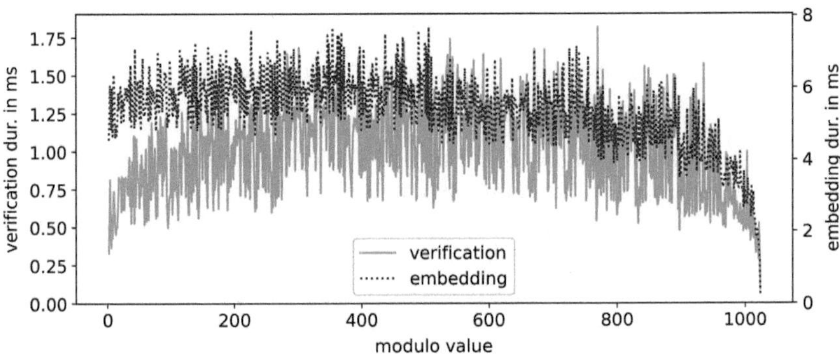

Fig. 6.15 Duration for different m during RDMC of 10-bit modulo-m counter

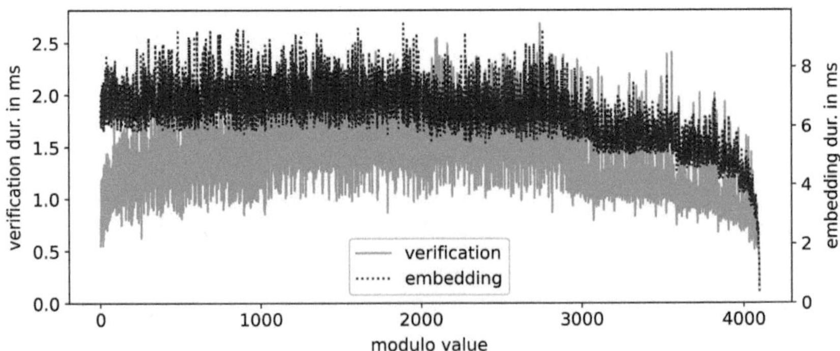

Fig. 6.16 Duration for different m during RDMC of 12-bit modulo-m counter

Further, the number of garbage outputs has been measured. The results for an 8-bit modulo counter and modulo values $1 < m \leq 256$ are shown in Fig. 6.17. The number of garbage outputs added by the RDMC-half-embedding are marked with crosses. The minimal value $\lceil log_2(M) \rceil$ named in Sect. 3.5, is given as circles. Lastly, the n garbage outputs added by the BDD-based method of [21], are shown as squares. The following can be observed when analyzing those results:

- The graphs for the number of added garbage outputs and for the minimal value are equal, even though RDMC-half-embedding does not always compute an optimal embedding, as discussed in Sect. 5.2. But with modulo counters, for all current states q mapped to an equal successor state holds $m \leq q < 2^n$ for some modulo value m. Hence, the number of different variable assignments in those current states, which decides the number of added outputs, is equal to $\lceil log_2(M) \rceil$.
- For $m \leq 128$ all graphs are equal, but for the remaining values RDMC-half-embedding adds less garbage outputs. This improvement increases for higher values of m. Hence, adding garbage outputs based on RDMC is definitely profitable for the verification of modulo counters.

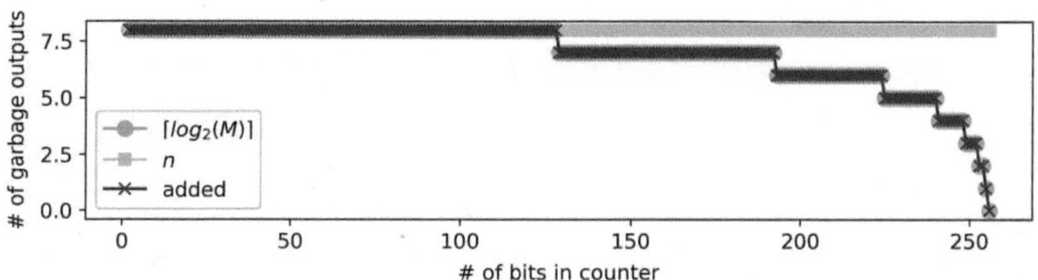

Fig. 6.17 Garbage outputs for different m during RDMC of 8-bit modulo-m counter

Very similar results can be seen in Fig. 6.18 for $n = 4$, in Fig. 6.19 for $n = 6$, in Fig. 6.20 for $n = 10$ and in Fig. 6.21 for $n = 14$.

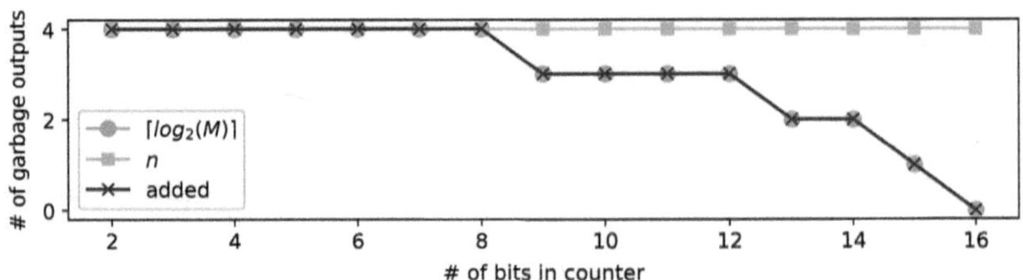

Fig. 6.18 Garbage outputs for different m during RDMC of 4-bit modulo-m counter

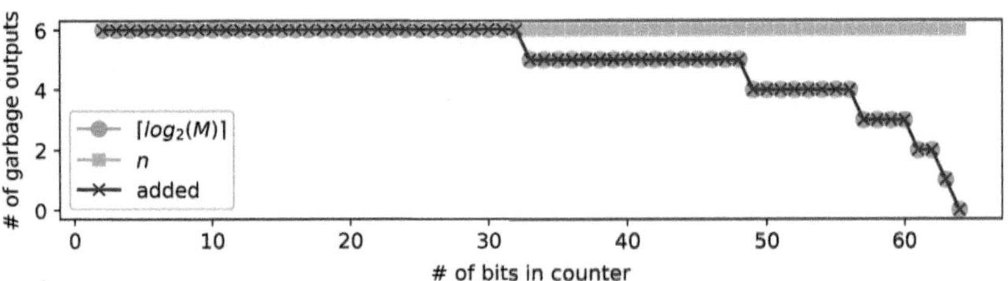

Fig. 6.19 Garbage outputs for different m during RDMC of 6-bit modulo-m counter

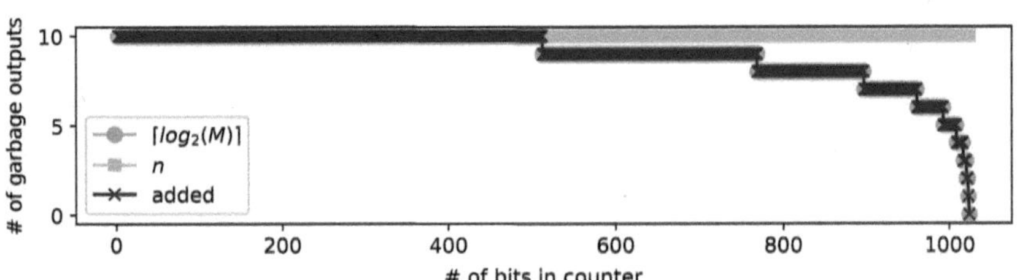

Fig. 6.20 Garbage outputs for different m during RDMC of 10-bit modulo-m counter

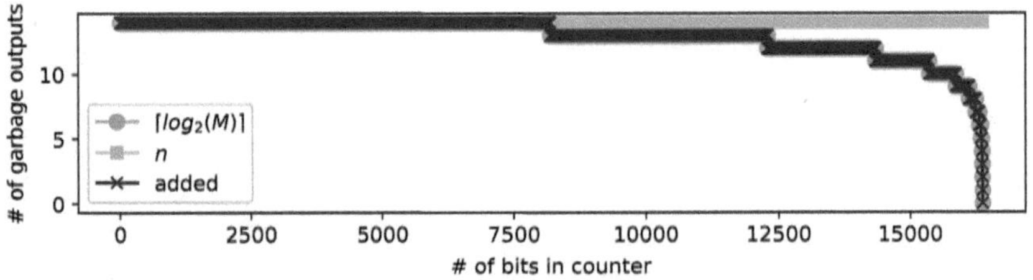

Fig. 6.21 Garbage outputs for different m during RDMC of 14-bit modulo-m counter

6.2.2   Fixed Modulo Value

As a second step, the implementation was executed for a fixed modulo value m and the number of variables n was varied. This way it is possible to analyze examples with higher values than $n = 14$, because not all values m have to be calculated. Further, the growth of any measured value with respect to n can be analyzed.

The value for m was chosen based on the measurements of Sect. 6.2.1. E.g. for the values $130 \leq m \leq 190$, the 8-bit mod-m counter in Fig. 6.6 has the highest measured BDD sizes. This range for m is therefore representative of the more demanding cases and hence useful for experiments. Generalized to any n this range is $2^{n-1} + 2 \leq m \leq 2^n - 2^{n-2} - 2$.

The specific value $m = 2^{n-1} + 2$ was chosen and executed for all values $0 < n \leq 30$. The resulting BDD sizes measured can be seen in Fig. 6.22. Like before, $|T|$ is shown as squares, $|he(T)|$ as circles and the peak in size of intermediate BDDs during the verification as crosses and during the embedding as triangles. The upper bound for $|he(T)|$ given in Lemma 5.4 as $2 \cdot (|T| + n)$, was again added as a dashed line and is never exceeded. In general, these results are similar to the observations of the experiments in Sect. 6.2.1, and confirm them for higher n.

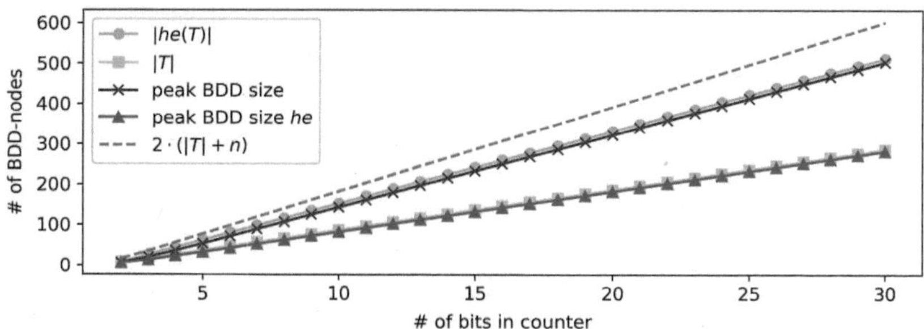

Fig. 6.22 BDD sizes for different n and $m = 2^{n-1} + 2$ during RDMC of n-bit modulo-m counter

The corresponding runtime of each execution is visualized in Fig. 6.23. The time was measured in milliseconds, the duration of the RDMC-based half embedding is shown as a solid line and the duration of the verification as a dotted line. This overall does not exceed 20 milliseconds and is hence still efficient for higher n. Again, a reference function $a \cdot n^2$ with $a = 0.009$ was added as a dashed line. This supports the statements of Theorem 5.1 and Theorem 5.2 that the runtime grows polynomially with respect to n.

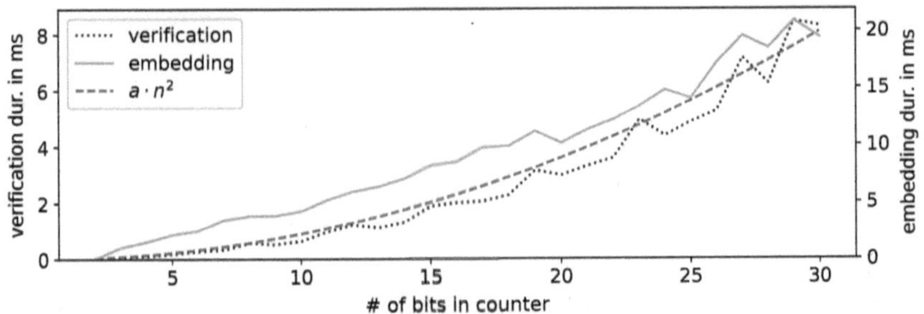

Fig. 6.23 Duration for different n and $m = 2^{n-1} + 2$ during RDMC of n-bit modulo-m counter

This experiment has been repeated for different values of m to make the observations of this section more robust. The results for $m = 5$ can be seen in Fig. 6.24 and in Fig. 6.25, for $m = 2^n - 5$ in in Fig. 6.26 and Fig. 6.27 and for $m = 2^{n-3} + 7$ in Fig. 6.28 and in Fig. 6.29. As the results are very similar, they are not analyzed in detail here.

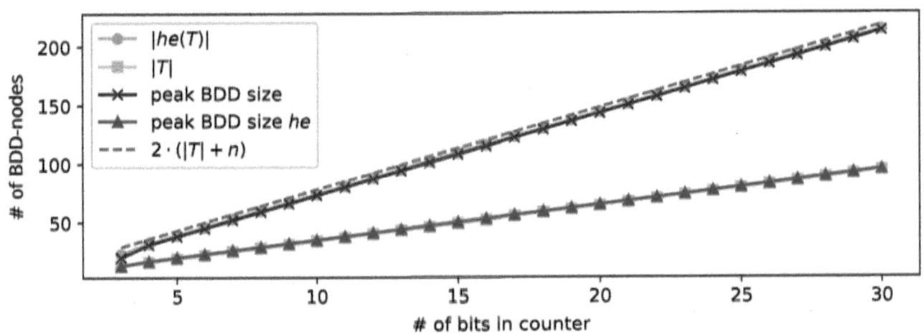

Fig. 6.24 BDD sizes for different n during RDMC of n-bit modulo-5 counter

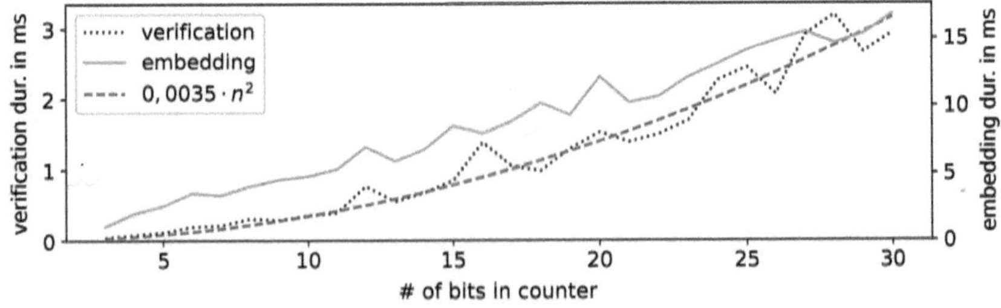

Fig. 6.25 Duration for different n during RDMC of n-bit modulo-5 counter

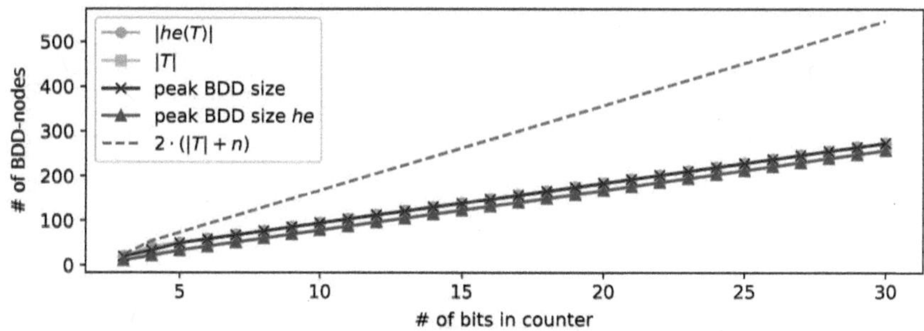

Fig. 6.26 BDD sizes for different n during RDMC of n-bit modulo-$(2^n - 5)$ counter

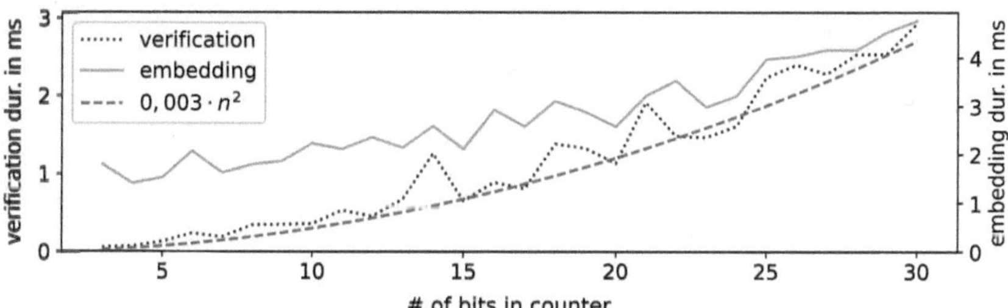

Fig. 6.27 Duration for different n during RDMC of n-bit modulo-$(2^n - 5)$ counter

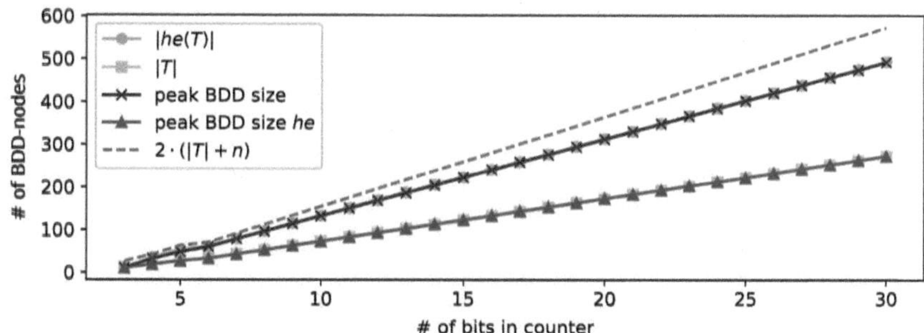

Fig. 6.28 BDD sizes for different n during RDMC of n-bit modulo-$(2^{n-3} + 7)$ counter

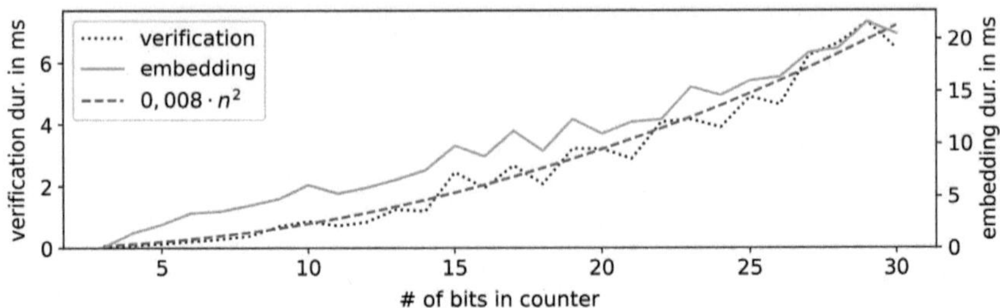

Fig. 6.29 Duration for different n during RDMC of n-bit modulo-$(2^{n-3} + 7)$ counter

Conclusion 7

In this final section, the results of this thesis are reviewed and possible future directions are discussed.

The main goal of this thesis was to propose a method for the efficient formal verification of sequential circuits with an exponential sequential depth. This was achieved for the first time, by proving polynomial upper bounds for the formal verification of different counter circuits, based on the following steps:

- With RDMC a model checking variant was presented, with which PFV could be proven for n-bit full counter circuits despite their exponential sequential depth.
- Since RDMC is mainly applicable to circuits, that compute a bijective function, the procedure was extended. Based on the concept of embedding, which is originally used in the domain of reversible computation, RDMC-based half embedding was proposed to modify non-bijective functions so that RDMC can be applied.
- Using a combination of RDMC-half-embedding and RDMC, PFV could be proven for any n-bit modulo-m counter as well.

The experiments implementing this combined approach are extremely promising. The established method could only verify a 30-bit full counter within a 3 hour timeout, the computations for all benchmarks containing more state bits did not terminate in time. But even a 1024-bit full counter could be verified with RDMC in about 30 seconds. The experiments for modulo counters are equally efficient.

C. Dominik, *Embedding Sequential Circuits for their Polynomial Formal Verification*, BestMasters, https://doi.org/10.1007/978-3-658-50155-6_7

7.1   Future Directions

There are still many open challenges left in the area of PFV. The accomplishments
for combinational circuits listed in Chap. 2 are yet to be extended to be applicable
to larger classes of circuits. Especially processors with a broader set of instructions
are of interest. But even more open questions could be analyzed with regard to PFV
of sequential circuits, as research on this topic has only just started. This includes
e.g. analyzing processors with a pipeline.

Specifically considering the results of this thesis, two directions for future
research are explained in the following.

7.1.1   RDMC-Based Full Embedding

The method proposed in Definition 5.2 for RDMC-based half embedding specifically aims to modify non-bijective functions, so that RDMC can be applied. But the
method could be extended with regard to reversible computation. The BDD-based
embedding method of [21] described in Sect. 3.5 does not only add garbage outputs,
but constant inputs as well. For such a full embedding based on RDMC the same
procedure for adding constant inputs could not directly be applied. But whenever
RDMC-full-embedding reduces the number of garbage outputs compared to the
method of [21], a reduction of constant inputs could be possible as well. Further,
the resulting, embedded function could then be used to derive a sequential circuit.

7.1.2   Application to Other Circuits

To give this thesis a reasonable framing, specific case studies for sequential circuits
were chosen. A focus was set on proving PFV for full counters and modulo counters.
But those results cannot directly be applied to other circuits with an exponential
sequential depth. The two main reasons for this are explained in the following:

- If the BDD representing the transition relation T has a size, that is exponential
  with respect to the number of state bits n, the required resources will be exponential as well. This can often be influenced by the variable order, consider e.g. the
  functions in Example 3.2 and Example 4.6. There it can easily be seen that it is
  most effective to keep variables, that depend on each other, as closely together as
  possible. But for some functions, like multiplication, no BDD with polynomial

size can be constructed [16]. Both, finding a suitable variable order or proving that there is none, require a manual analysis of the circuit, that is to be verified.

- Another aspect that requires manual effort, is determining the resources needed for the operation "$\exists$". In Theorem 5.1 polynomial upper bounds were proven for the half embedding of modulo counters. This proof was based on the restriction that the quantification step $\exists S$ was applied going from s_0 to s_{n-1}. Then, the result of each quantification is not bigger than the baseline BDD T, which proves that there is no blow-up in size. Now, if the application order is altered to going top down from s_{n-1} to s_0, some intermediate results of $\exists S$ can be bigger than T. This increase in size is not significant enough to affect the overall polynomial runtime, but it shows how complicated it is to predict which operations can be applied efficiently. Narrowing down general properties for a BDD, that ensure an existential quantification cannot (significantly) increase its size, is tricky.

It is desirable in future research to define more generic properties for circuits, which behave well when RDMC or RDMC-based half embedding is applied. They could then be used to prove PFV for other classes of circuits with an exponential sequential depth. A first step would be to analyze more complex counter circuits, e.g. counters with a reset input. But of course a variety of sequential circuits is of interest. The behavior of the proposed algorithm could be tried on established benchmarks for sequential circuits for a start.

Even though numerous questions for future research remain, this thesis leads to a strongly positive conclusion. The concept of embedding could successfully be adapted to the domain of PFV. Based on this, the theoretical and experimental results satisfy the goal of an efficient verification of full counter circuits and modulo counter circuits. The approach of combining RDMC and RDMC-based half embedding further gives a promising foundation for the PFV of sequential circuits.

References

1. D. Brand, "Verification of large synthesized designs," in *International Conference on Computer Aided Design*, 1993, pp. 534–537.
2. R. Brinkmann and D. Kelf, "Formal verification—the industrial perspective," in *Formal System Verification: State-of the-Art and Future Trends*, R. Drechsler, Ed. Springer Cham, 2018, pp. 155–182.
3. S. A. Cook, "The complexity of theorem-proving procedures," in *ACM Symposium on Theory of Computing*, 1971, pp. 151–158.
4. E. M. Clarke, T. A. Henzinger, H. Veith, and R. Bloem, *Handbook of Model Checking*. Springer Cham, 2018.
5. R. Drechsler, "PolyAdd: Polynomial formal verification of adder circuits," in *International Symposium on Design and Diagnostics of Electronic Circuits & Systems*, 2021, pp. 99–104.
6. L. Müller and R. Drechsler, "SAT can ensure polynomial bounds for the verification of circuits with limited cutwidth," in *Euromicro Conference on Digital System Design*, 2024, pp. 57–64.
7. M. Nadeem, C. K. Jha, and R. Drechsler, "Polynomial formal verification of approximate adders with constant cutwidth," in *IEEE European Test Symposium*, 2024, pp. 1–6.
8. R. Drechsler, A. Mahzoon, and M. Goli, "Towards polynomial formal verification of complex arithmetic circuits," in *International Symposium on Design and Diagnostics of Electronic Circuits & Systems*, 2022.
9. J. Kleinekathöfer, A. Mahzoon, and R. Drechsler, "Polynomial formal verification of floating point adders," in *Design, Automation & Test in Europe Conference & Exhibition*, 2023, pp. 1–2.
10. L. Weingarten, K. Datta, A. Kole, and R. Drechsler, "Complete and efficient verification for a RISC-V processor using formal verification," in *Design, Automation & Test in Europe Conference & Exhibition*, 2024.
11. C. Dominik and R. Drechsler, "Polynomial formal verification of sequential circuits," in *Design, Automation & Test in Europe Conference & Exhibition*, 2024.
12. R. Wille and R. Drechsler, *Towards a Design Flow for Reversible Logic*. Springer Dordrecht, 2010.
13. R. Landauer, "Irreversibility and heat generation in the computing process," in *IBM Journal of Research and Development*, 1961, pp. 183–191.

C. Dominik, *Embedding Sequential Circuits for their Polynomial Formal Verification*, BestMasters, https://doi.org/10.1007/978-3-658-50155-6

14. C. H. Bennett, "Logical reversibility of computation," in *IBM Journal of Research and Development*, 1973, pp. 525–532.
15. R. E. Bryant, "Symbolic simulation-techniques and applications," in ACM/IEEE *Design Automation Conference*, 1990, pp. 517–521.
16. R. E. Bryant, "Graph-based algorithms for Boolean function manipulation," in *IEEE Transactions on Computers*, vol. 35, no. 8, 1986, pp. 677–691.
17. R. E. Bryant and Y.-A. Chen, "Verification of arithmetic circuits with binary moment diagrams*," in *32nd Design Automation Conference*, 1995, pp. 535–541.
18. R. Drechsler and M. Schnieber, "Next-generation automatic humanreadable proofs enabling polynomial formal verification," in *International Symposium on Formal Methods and Models for System Design*, 2023, pp. 122–125.
19. M. Keim, M. Martin, B. Becker, R. Drechsler, and P. Molitor, "Polynomial formal verification of multipliers," in *IEEE VLSI Test Symposium*, 1997, pp. 150–155.
20. D. Maslov and G. W. Dueck, "Reversible cascades with minimal garbage," in *IEEE Transactions on Computer-Aided Design of Integrated Circuits and Systems*, 2004, pp. 1497–1509.
21. M. Soeken, R. Wille, O. Keszocze, D. M. Miller, and R. Drechsler, "Embedding of large Boolean functions for reversible logic," in *ACM Journal on Emerging Technologies in Computing Systems*, 2014, pp. 1–26.
22. C. H. Bennett, "Logical reversibility of computation," in *IBM Journal of Research and Development*, 1973, pp. 525–532.
23. F. Somenzi, "CUDD: CU decision diagram package release 3.0.0," 2016. [Online]. Available: https://github.com/ivmai/cudd